MW01236354

"*The Praying Youth Ministry* will be my go-to book for youth leaders. The style is very readable. It's profusely biblically, and also very practical. Mike Higgs has created a gem."

—*Doug Clark, National Field Director, the National Network of Youth Ministries*

"*The Praying Youth Ministry* is a must read for any believer concerned about the next generation on any level. Mike has legitimately made the case for a re-formation of youth ministry, beginning with a leader sincerely committing to cultivate an authentic relationship with God through prayer—and then modeling that pursuit for the young people they lead. I agree with Mike wholeheartedly that the fuel for revival is prayer. This book provides the inspiration for change, as well as practical recommendations to apply right away."

—*Debbie Bresina, President, Dare 2 Share*

"Our defenses sound the alarm if told our precious youth minis-tries *should* step up prayer. '*Why?*' we demand, and the reasons better be convincing. Alternately, someone might reassure us that our youth ministry *can* improve at prayer. In that case, our more relaxed, curious question is '*how?*' Mike Higgs answers both questions with the seasoned wisdom of an original gangster in youth ministry. Youth ministry can pivot from today's fruit-feeble, resource-rich, program-based models to centering around the living presence of Jesus Christ. (NYC youth minister Keithen Schwahn testifies about this during one heart-pumping chapter!) Higgs drew upon uncommonly cherished prayer to write these words. Profoundly simple. Deeply life-giving. Why not join our Fellowship of Facelessness? May this book provoke you to pray and obey for youth ministry's glorious upgrade."

—*Dave Rahn, PhD, Senior Advisor, The TENx10 Collaboration*

"One thing you can count on with my good friend, Mike Higgs, he lives the message of this book. He and I have walked side-by-side on the 'youth ministry adventure' for four decades, and early on we shared our common passion for 'the praying youth ministry'—long before a book was in the works. We began praying together with a small group of youth leaders at a retreat in Colorado, and later we were on the National Prayer Committee together, but most importantly . . . we have shared the common vision and burden that the only way the younger generation culture will change, either in a person, youth group or church, is to experience a 'Jesus revolution' through in-depth, lasting, disciple-making youth ministry ignited by a 'Pray with Passion' fire in the hearts of pastors, parents, youth leaders and students."

—*Barry St. Clair, Vice President, Global Youth Engagement, East-West*

"The youth leader who wants fresh ideas to 'get prayer going' in a student group will be drawn to *The Praying Youth Ministry*. That makes sense since the book contains more immediately useable prayer ideas than any book I have seen. The ideas are valuable and worth much more than the cost of the book. Even so, these excellent ideas are not the most essential elements of this important book. Even more valuable is the attention that Mike gives to the life of the youth leader. Higgs correctly suggests that personal holiness and purity are the most important prerequisites to prevailing prayer. He then points to the powerful influence of a leader who models a lifestyle of prayer. Only when purity and modeling are in place does he focus on mobilizing prayer initiatives. Mike Higgs has coordinated more multidenominational, national prayer initiatives than almost anyone. Those of us who know him best know that public stature flows from a pure life and modeling a deep life of prayer. He was just the one to write this important book."

—*Richard Ross, Ph.D., senior professor of student ministry, Southwestern Seminary*

"Mike's life and voice are the rarest of gifts to the Body of Christ. His pedigree of experience leading youth ministry locally, regionally, and nationally, is unlike anyone I've ever met in 30 years of leadership. His is a voice in the wilderness that needs to be heard by modern-day youth ministry practitioners. Mike is a personal mentor and when he speaks, I listen. I hope you listen carefully to the important message found within *The Praying Youth Ministry*."

—*Geoff Eckart, CEO, Never The Same and Claim Your Campus, Chairman of America's National Prayer Committee*

"Most of us know the future of the American church depends upon a rising generation who know how to pray. Our problem is we tend not to know how to nurture that generation. We've often tried the simple quick fixes. We've sometimes tried the intensives. And sadly, all too often the results haven't been great. What I like about *The Praying Youth Ministry* is that it isn't a quick fix. It is reflections based on 40+ years of experience. Nor is it over-intense. It is full of realism, practicality and above all, hope. It meets you and your ministry right where you are and gives pointers on how to go further on and deeper in to the Father in prayer. Refreshing, inspiring and insightful."

—*Colin Piper, NxtMove/World Evangelical Alliance*

"*The Praying Youth Ministry* is a must read for every person with a heart for the rising generation. This book will help leaders prioritize presence over program, allowing youth to truly experience Jesus in a way that ignites their passions for seeing the kingdom of God and the good news of the gospel spread among their peers. Mike weaves together a beautiful picture of prioritizing character in our own lives, teaching students to pray, and a biblical understanding of the importance of corporate prayer. I've had the privilege of walking with Mike for over 30 years in ministry, and have experienced with him the stories shared in this book. He has modeled what he teaches, and has mentored and taught me how to mobilize prayer. This book will not only inspire you to lead through prayer, but will give you practical help along the way."

—*Renee Boucher, Western States Regional Director, 24-7 Prayer USA*

THE
PRAYING
YOUTH
MINISTRY

LEADING
& MINISTERING
FROM UPPER ROOMS

MIKE HIGGS

WITH

Jarin Oda, Keithen Schwahn, Phil Togwell
and Olivia Williamson

PRAYERSHOP
PUBLISHING
Terre Haute, Indiana

PrayerShop Publishing is the publishing arm of the Church Prayer Leaders Network. The Church Prayer Leaders Network exists to equip and inspire local churches and prayer leaders in their desire to disciple people in prayer and to become a "house of prayer for all nations." Its online store, prayershop.org, offers more than 150 prayer resources for purchase or download.

ISBN (Print): 978-1-970176-31-5
ISBN (E-Book): 978-1-970176-32-2

All Scripture quotations, unless otherwise indicated, are taken from the Holy Bible, *New International Version*,® *NIV*.® Copyright © 1973, 1978, 1984 by Biblica, Inc.® Used by permission. All rights reserved worldwide.

Printed in the United States of America

Acknowledgments

NOT LONG AGO my wife, Terri, and I talked at dinner about how the themes of two of my books—*Youth Ministry from the Inside Out* (character), and *Youth Ministry on Your Knees* (prayer)—seem as relevant and needed today as when I wrote them more than 20 years ago. However, getting the message of two out-of-print books into the hands of today's youth workers seemed elusive. So, our conversation turned into a prayer. Literally the next day, an email arrived from Jon Graf, publisher of PrayerShop Publishing, with an invitation to write this book. Thanks, Jon. And sorry, Lemon Oreos are just plain wrong.

Thanks to the men who, over the years, have taught me how to walk with God and how to pray. Dan Pitney fed me spiritual milk and baby food as a new believer. Gary Casady saw and nurtured the hidden youth worker in me. Terry Dirks, Chuck Pierce, Eddie Smith, Steve Hawthorne, Gary Bergel, David Bryant and Joe Aldrich, seasoned prayer leaders with global influence, invested in me personally. Someone once aptly called humility "the elusive virtue," and these believers incarnated Christlikeness and a devotion to prayer in a spirit of humility. Their examples have marked me for life.

Tim Rohrer and Mark Jones have been scary accurate prophetic voices whom God has used in my life for many decades, to impart life-changing truths as well as life-altering ministry trajectories. Thank you for being His instruments.

Renee Boucher has laughed, cried, and prayed with me through many of the stories in this book. Thank you for your enduring friendship.

Also, thanks to the Upper Room Practitioners writers—Jarin Oda, Keithen Schwahn, Phil Togwell, and Olivia Williamson—whose lives and ministries we all can learn from, no matter what our age or experience.

It has been my great joy to be involved in both the International House of Prayer Kansas City (IHOP-KC) and 24-7 Prayer movements since their early years. David Sliker (IHOP-KC) and David Blackwell (24-7 Prayer), thanks for the introductions and making me feel welcome in your "families."

I especially thank my wife, Terri, the most devout woman I've ever known, and whose prayer life influenced this book more than any other person.

Finally, and most of all, thanks to the Lover of My Soul, Jesus, who informed every word that follows.

MIKE HIGGS

Contents

Part Three

THE UPPER ROOM OF ACTS: CORPORATE PRAYER   *117*

The Upper Rooms

FOR 15 YEARS of local church youth pastoring, I considered prayer a primary value in my ministry philosophy. After I burned out (more on that later) and transitioned to the nonprofit youth ministry world, prayer grew into a primary expression of my ministry.

I mobilized prayer for local, regional, and national youth ministry events for close to 25 years. Sometimes I recruited teams of intercessors to show up on site and pray for eight to 12 hours a day for the duration of an event (which was, and is, crazy).

On other occasions, I served as the roving prayer guy, supporting speakers, musicians, and volunteers through intercession in green rooms and hotel suites. I've trained students in prayer in conference seminars, and curated prayer rooms where students stood in line up to 45 minutes to get maybe three to four minutes of personal prayer and perhaps a prophetic word from gifted leaders. I've facilitated prayer summits for youth workers where the agenda was no agenda, other than to pray.

While I'm in a different season of life now, and don't engage in as much of that as I used to, stories from those halcyon days (as well as present days) are scattered throughout this book. But my point here at the start: the reason prayer was a primary value for me as a youth pastor, and the reason I ended up doing prayer mobilization, was not because I was particularly good or gifted at prayer. I learned as I went. I made ample mistakes, and was mentored my some amazing people. But for reasons that to this day are not entirely clear, I understood early on that when Jesus said, ". . . apart from Me, you can do nothing" (Jn. 15:5), He meant it.

Accordingly, I have always understood the importance of prayer and have been willing to go all in with it. Similarly, I'm writing this book to cajole my tribe of youth workers to do likewise. This book isn't just a resource to help youth workers add prayer to their arsenal of ministry tools. This is a call to desperate, prevailing prayer because, as you will read, I believe the times demand it.

The Evolving Themes

My framework is complicit in the book's subtitle: Upper Rooms. It didn't start that way. My original intent was to do a radical re-write and update of my book, *Youth Ministry on Your Knees*. But God hijacked my intentions in an interesting way.

On the morning I began writing, I realized that during the previous night, God had spoken to me about three different kinds of **upper rooms.** I don't know when or how this happened. I've no recollection of a dream or vision or divine encounter. Yes, my Bible reading had just taken me through the last part of the Gospel of John and the first part of Acts, where upper rooms are prominent in the narratives. Still, before that morning I didn't make the connections I am going to unpack in the pages that follow.

The three upper rooms are:

The Upper Room of **Prayer Prerequisites.** While my Bible is not marked up like some I've seen, with the text almost obscured by highlighting and notes, I've used colored pencils liberally over the years, including highlighting in green every passage that mentions prayer, either directly or indirectly. The previous morning, when reading John 13 through 17, known as the Upper Room Discourse, I had noticed more than a few passages highlighted in green pencil, most with a common theme: prayer prerequisites. While not directly related to prayer, they are very much related to how we are to live our lives so that we are praying effectually (i.e. abiding, obedience, faith, etc.).

The Upper Room of **Personal Prayer.** Most are likely familiar with the Daniel, chapter 6 story of "Daniel and the lion's den" from Sunday School or Vacation Bible School. What we might not be as familiar with is how Daniel responded when King Darius the Mede was provoked into issuing a decree that stated, basically, anyone who prays to any god or man other than Darius is lunch for the lions. The passage says, "Now when Daniel learned that the decree has been published, he went home to his upstairs room . . . and prayed . . ." (vs. 10). It's a great example of personal prayer.

The Upper Room of **Corporate Prayer.** During the COVID pandemic, author and pastor Mark Batterson's National Community Church in Washington, D.C. held regular "Upper Zoom" prayer meetings online using Zoom software. Were they the first to use that phrase? No clue, but it is a clever play on words, and I quickly adopted the concept and regularly participate in "upper zoom" group prayer sessions. Most of us understand that Acts, chapters one and two, serve as the biblical reference for this group practice, where early believers followed Jesus' instructions and "all joined together constantly in prayer" (1:14).

Goals for This Book

In the following chapters I'll flesh out the framework of those three upper room concepts by exploring many facets of prayer. But beyond that framework, it's important to understand my goals for this book. Otherwise, you may find yourself wondering early on, "What does this have to do with prayer?" So here you go:

Ministry Re-formation. *To show that youth ministry re-formation is essential if we're to fulfill our mission of reaching the emerging generations.* And that re-formation begins, and is sustained, with prevailing prayer. If you want a primer just on prayer, check the Appendix, where I've listed some excellent books. If you want a text on youth ministry praxis, they abound. But if you're desperate for more of God in your life, and long to see youth ministry fulfill its destiny as an agent of spiritual awakening among the emerging generations, keep reading.

Godly Character. *To make a compelling case that character—personal holiness and purity—is the most important prerequisite to prevailing prayer.* Spoiler alert: I'm going to point out that personal holiness hasn't been a great strength in youth ministry, and this needs to change. Growing a praying youth ministry starts at the top with the youth worker. "A student is not above his teacher, but everyone who is fully trained will be like his teacher" (Lk. 6:40). For this reason, there will be more content on character, holiness, purity, and the personal prayer life of youth workers than simply stuff on "how to get the kids in your youth group praying." If the former happens, the latter happens.

Prayer for Everyone. *To de-mystify prayer.* Far too many times, I've shown up at an event and heard the following: "I'm sure glad you're here. I'm not very good at prayer, and we certainly need prayer." There are a number of fallacies in that statement, and I want to point them out. Mighty, prevailing prayer is for everyone.

Effective Resources. *To offer resources and helps for those of the youth ministry tribe who desire to make an "all in" commitment to personal and ministry prayer.* In this regard, I'll pull from personal experiences, the wisdom of folks currently practicing innovative and radical prayer, and from the vast library of books published by prayer warriors over the years.

I bring strengths and weaknesses to writing this book. I'm not the next intercessory incarnation of great prayer-ers like George Mueller or Rees Howell, nor does my character match the piety of a Brother Lawrence, Thomas à Kempis, or John Wesley. But I've been mentored in prayer by godly people. I've had the privilege of swimming in many different streams of the prayer movement. I've served on America's National Prayer Committee for more than 25 years. I've decades of exposure to, and involvement with, both the 24-7 Prayer movement and IHOP-KC. I've led many prayer teams, and have been wrecked before God, on my face, in too many venues to remember, much less mention. And although I'm no longer "in the trenches" of daily interaction with teenagers, I'm still engaged in youth ministry work and still call youth workers my tribe.

On the other hand, while I may practice intercessory prayer more than many, I don't think of myself as an intercessor, per se. That term doesn't appear in New Testament spiritual gifts lists, although the book, *Your Spiritual Gifts Can Help Your Church Grow* by C. Peter Wagner (Regal Books, 2012), lists it as a gift and makes a good supporting argument. Legitimate spiritual gift or not, this much I know: I'm married to an intercessor, and I can't match her fervency or frequency. Some make a distinction between intercessors and prayer mobilizers; if that is true, I'm probably more of the latter than the former.

To summarize: I do have some experience and, hopefully, wisdom to share. Perhaps even some knowledge that can help youth leaders building praying youth ministries. And in recognition that I have not been "in the trenches" for a while, I've also included the insights of practicing youth leaders. You'll find them in the first Selah: Upper Room Practitioners', young(er) members of our tribe doing cool stuff in the realm of prayer.

So, buckle up. Here we go.

PART ONE

The Upper Room of the Last Supper: Prayer Prerequisites

I LOVE THE SERIES, *The Chosen*. Terri and I have watched every episode multiple times. Good stuff! I love how the movie portrays biblical characters. While there is no direct biblical evidence that Matthew struggled with Asperger's Syndrome and lived as a New Testament equivalent of Elon Musk—both different and brilliant—the attention to detail in his Gospel fits his portrayal in the show. Now John's character in *The Chosen* especially aligns with my mental image of one of the Sons of Thunder. He exudes passion in his Gospel, his three epistles, and most certainly in Revelation. I'm thankful John also gives attention to detail in The Upper Room Discourse (Jn. 13-17), his account of Jesus' last time with the Apostles before His arrest and crucifixion.

The discourse began in an upper room, which other gospel writers identify as the place where they celebrated the Passover Feast. (The iconic Last Supper painting by Leonardo da Vinci might come to mind). Two chapters into his discourse, Jesus pauses in the midst of His final teachings to announce, "Come now; let us leave" (14:31). The three chapters that follow are almost entirely red letters, the words of Jesus to His followers while walking with them from the upper room to Gethsemane.

The Upper Room Discourse is a very weighty passage; almost every verse seems to carry a profound truth. When my daily Bible reading took me there not long ago, I looked forward to more profundity. But something different caught me by surprise. Like I wrote in the introduction, I've marked up my Bible, including highlighting in green every verse and passage that, directly or indirectly, addresses prayer. Because of this, as I began reading John 13, I realized the Upper Room Discourse has a lot more to say about prayer, or more specifically prerequisites to prayer, than I had realized.

It's hard to overemphasize the importance of these prayer prerequisites. This is true (as we will see) when it comes to both personal prayer–how you spend your time alone with God–as well as corporate prayer–how you disciple your youth group in prayer. I believe prayer prerequisites are *the* key to effective prayer. "The prayer of a righteous man is powerful and effective" (Jas. 5:16). "If you remain in Me, and My words remain in you, ask whatever you wish, and it will be done for you" (Jn. 15:7).

So please, please, don't skip this section. This book focuses on developing a praying youth ministry, and our ministries won't become prayer powerhouses ushering in youth ministry re-for-mation and spiritual awakening among the emerging generations (something we can all agree is desperately needed!) unless we grapple with the prerequisites.

Chapter 1

Youth Ministry Re-formation

And no one pours new wine into old wineskins. If he does,
the new wine will burst the skins, the wine will run out
and the wineskins will be ruined. No, new wine must be
poured into new wineskins.

—LUKE 5:37

IN MY TWENTIES I worked as a fledgling sports reporter for my city's daily newspaper while moonlighting as a freelance writer. The church I attended started up a new high school ministry and needed the requisite guitar-playing song leader. That was my gig in college, so they recruited me to help out. Four months later I was an intern at the church, enrolled in seminary, and in training to become a youth pastor. Yikes. I didn't see that one coming as a viable career trajectory.

Over four decades later, I think I'm still a youth worker, at least at heart. I lasted 15 years as a youth pastor before a nasty burnout precipitated a transition that led me into the nonprofit world. Since then, I've mentored and networked youth workers, written some books, and served as a prayer mobilizer for a variety of local and national initiatives and events. More recently, God has diversified my portfolio—I now run a Chamber of Commerce (I know, I don't get it, either), serve as a county chaplain, and am immersed in civic affairs. My wife and I operate a private retreat house in the middle of nowhere in Idaho, and we recently launched the Hailey House of Prayer with a team of 16.

A Growing Unease

While I spend an increasing amount of time outside the genre, I still love youth ministry. Youth workers are still my tribe, and my passion to disciple the emerging generations burns as strong as ever. However, I acknowledge a subtle but persistent growing unease regarding the effectiveness of contemporary/postmodern/missional/ COVID-impacted youth ministry (pick one or more labels) at making disciples among the emerging generations. I can't shake the nagging feeling that *there must be more,* and that a prayer-driven *re-formation* is desperately needed in youth ministry praxis. Increasingly, credible research supports my uneasiness.

The late Mike Yaconelli, co-founder with Wayne Rice of Youth Specialties in the late 1960s, is remembered by many as "the godfather of modern youth ministry." Edgy and provocative, while at the same time kind-hearted, Mike was a prophetic voice in a movement to adolescents that was entering its own adolescent phase. In June 2003, Yaconelli wrote one of his last columns, entitled "The Failure of Youth Ministry" (*Youth Worker Journal,* 2003). His column concluded like this:

> So, let's be honest.
>
> Youth ministry as an experiment has failed. If we want to see the church survive, we need to rethink youth ministry.
>
> What does that mean? I don't have a clue. But my hunch is that if we want to see young people have a faith that lasts, then we have to completely change the way we do youth ministry in America.
>
> I wonder if any of us has the courage to try.

Yaconelli wrote a follow-up column called "An Apology," where he admitted to some overreach and hyperbole in his comments.

But I do believe there was—and is—a prophetic accuracy in the closing wake-up call of his column: *"…we have to completely change the way we do youth ministry in America."*

A Brief History of Youth Ministry

While youth ministry per se can't be found in the Bible, the essence of youth ministry—preaching the Gospel of Jesus, advancing the Kingdom of God on earth, and making disciples among an unreached generation—is as biblical as baptism. Running on the timeless and tested tracks of relational, incarnational ministry, God clearly raised up youth ministry for a season in history, and that season has endured. But will it continue?

A short crash-course on the history of youth ministry will be helpful here. What follows will be brief and to the point. Smart people have written entire dissertations and books on this subject, good ones at that. And yes, we will return to prayer, eventually. This just lays some necessary groundwork.

We have some anecdotal evidence, going back to the 18th and 19th Centuries, or people in the church being assigned to minister to the children or youth in their congregations. One could make a strong argument that the American public school system, (which began in churches!) and the venerable institution of Sunday School were both early prototypes of youth ministry.

In his book, *Teenage: The Prehistory of Youth Culture 1875-1945* (Penguin Books, 2008), John Savage traces the emergence of the descriptive term "teenager" back to around 1944, but as his title implies, teenagers didn't just appear on the scene unannounced. The length and depth of Savage's analysis—over 500 pages of text and notes—attests the emergence during his "prehistory" years of a distinct and significant adolescent age group within Western culture, and notably, in America. The spiritual significance of this "emerging people group" of sorts is underscored by the simultaneous emergence of ministries like the YMCA, Christian endeavor, Epworth League, Word of Life, and many other independent local and regional out-reaches God raised up to reach out to young people.

However, modern youth ministry likely began in the 1940s with the rise of the "big three" youth ministry organizations: Young Life (YL), Youth For Christ (YFC) and the Fellowship of Christian Athletes (FCA). My contention is God raised up these ministries, and subsequently many others like them, to reach a generation rendered spiritually, emotionally, and/or physically fatherless by World War 2, modern industrialization, and the myth of the American Dream. They also combatted the erosion of disciple-making as a foundational pillar of the faith.

In the 1950s and 60s, American "teenagers" came of age. As the late Beatle John Lennon said, "America used to be the big youth place in everybody's imagination. America had teenagers and everywhere else just had people." Correspondingly, Saturday night youth rallies and Bible clubs attracted huge crowds in many American cities, and millions from this new unreached people group of teenagers came to faith in Christ. The emergence of the Jesus People movement in the late 1960s and early 1970's–recently portrayed in the movie *Jesus Revolution*—had a profound impact on reaching teenagers, too.

By the early 1970s, local churches responded, "Hey, we need to get in on the action, too!" and started hiring youth pastors in earnest. (OK, don't get bothered, that last statement was a bit tongue-in-cheek.) Churches adopted and modified the attractional models employed by the parachurch organizations to fit local church youth groups. Competition, drama, humor-laced talks by charismatic youth leaders, live music, multimedia presentations, and even food (Burger Bash! All-You-Can-Eat Pizza! The World's Longest Banana Split!) drew crowds of young people to youth groups. As a result, their curious parents often ended up in church on Sunday mornings.

A Diminishing Impact

Because the attractional model of youth ministry was quite effective in leading kids to Christ, youth outreach programs took on more importance, with disciple-making taking a back seat to evangelism. But somewhere in the 1980s, church parents started asking, "Why is Youth Pastor Pete spending so much time with unchurched kids while our little cherubs are getting neglected?" Youth workers started being encouraged (or required) to spend less time doing evangelism and more time investing in church kids.

By the 1990s, the attractional method waned in popularity and effectiveness. Teenagers inside and outside the church were increasingly distracted by the plethora of available entertainment and activity options vying for their time and attention. Teens and their parents often grew too busy or otherwise preoccupied to regularly attend a midweek youth group or a Sunday morning church service. And when teenagers did find time to check out a youth group, they often found the program not all that compelling or relevant. The youth ministry flavor of Christianity didn't seem to provide enduring answers for anxiety, depression, fatherlessness, or a host of other adolescent maladies that the culture was fueling. Youth group attendance across the country began to decline, and soon the youth pastor was no longer the near-automatic second pastoral hire at churches.

As it always has, youth ministry adjusted. Youth groups added contemplative elements like candles and the resurrection of the acoustic guitar (can I hear a Kumbaya?). Short-term missions experiences rapidly grew in popularity. Youth workers began to give more attention to helping students develop a defendable biblical world view and incarnate it in "missional" living.

Thoughtful books like Chap Clark's *Hurt* and *Hurt 2.0* (Baker, 2004 and 2011), and Jeff Keuss' *Blur: A New Paradigm for Understanding Youth Culture* (Zondervan, 2014) explored the complexity of youth culture and the increasingly scary traumas of adolescent life in a postmodern world where family dysfunction is the norm. These authors helped us see that issues facing teens were far more complex, and daunting, than acne, dating problems, and poor self-esteem. But despite the well-intended and spiritually healthy adjustments, research such as David Kinnaman and Gabe Lyons' *unChristian* (Baker, 2012), Kinnaman's *You Lost Me* (Baker, 2016), Christian Smith's *Soul Searching: The Religious and Spiritual Lives of American Teenagers* (Oxford University Press, 2009), and Kenda Creasy Dean's *Almost Christian* (Oxford University Press, 2010) substantiated what many feared: youth ministry was struggled to maintain traction in discipling the generations.

State of the Union

Which brings us to the present. In 2016 The Barna Group (a well-known market research firm), issued a report, "The State of Youth Ministry." It concluded: "For the most part, youth ministry in the U.S. is stable and functioning effectively . . . if it ain't broke, don't fix it." However, many youth workers I've encountered *do* think something is amiss, especially several years and one global pandemic later. Unless I'm talking to the wrong leaders . . . I'm hearing that youth group attendance continues to decrease, and the youth pastor has migrated south from the second to the fourth hire (after worship pastor and children's pastor) at local churches. I don't sense that today's youth pastors carry the same I'm-in-it-for-the-long-haul mindset they did a few decades ago. I've met more than a few youth workers in their late 20s or early 30s who are frustrated and preparing to move on to church planting or the marketplace.

That said, I don't believe youth ministry has run its course, or worse, turned into a train wreck of a parody. God certainly hasn't forgotten young people. Nor have they forgotten Him. While mid-week youth group attendance may be low, Claim Your Campus (more on this later) and other student-led campus prayer movements report solid, even growing numbers. Young Life still packs their summer camps, as does FCA and other organizations. Youth evangelist Shane Pruitt had this to say in a Facebook post from July 2023: "I've been preaching Youth Camps for 15+ years. In the past, if 10% of the crowd made a spiritual decision for Christ, it would be seen as a movement of God. This Summer, it's been anywhere between 20% to 30% at the camps that I've preached at, so far! I'm telling ya that God is moving amongst Generation Z! To Him be the glory!"

And here's an illustration that is dated but still relevant: late December 2012, 16,000 teens and 20somethings—mostly college students—gathered in St. Louis for *Urbana 2012*, a student missions conference held by InterVarsity Christian Fellowship every three years. At the same time in Kansas City, 25,000 students attended the International House of Prayer Kansas City's *One Thing*. A week later, close to 65,000 students packed the Georgia Dome in Atlanta for *Passion 2013*. Do the math. Over 100,000 students gave up almost a week of their Christmas break to attend one of these conferences, which were anything but milquetoast. All boldly called attendees to radically follow Christ and commit their lives to His service. In addition, untold thousands of students attended other less-visible conferences around the country during the same time frame. Where did all these hair-on-fire-for-Jesus students come from? Just a few years earlier, most were involved in church youth groups.

All the chatter about teenagers bailing on their youth groups, churches, and faith is legitimate, but something spiritually significant still exists.

More than another Shift

We can't call youth ministry a train wreck—God remains at work in the emerging generations—but my conviction remains: we need more than a subtle shift to get back on God's tracks. While youth ministry has always done a pretty good job of adjusting to changes in adolescent life and youth culture, it is time for a significant, prayer-driven re-formation in which new wineskins of youth ministry emerge.

> "Jesus went through all the towns and villages, teaching in their synagogues, preaching the good news of the kingdom and healing every disease and sickness. When he saw the crowds, he had compassion on them, because they were harassed and helpless, like sheep without a shepherd. Then he said to his disciples, 'The harvest is plentiful but the workers are few. Ask the Lord of the harvest, therefore, to send out workers into his harvest field'" (Mt. 9:35-38).

This was one of my go-to passages when speaking on the importance of youth ministry, ever since I heard the late youth speaker Dawson McAllister unpack it in the context of this questions: "What would Jesus think if He walked on a high school campus today?" While it's hard to support a claim that any people group or generation has cornered the market on being "harassed and helpless, like sheep without a shepherd," (vs. 36) most any youth worker—or teacher or coach or parent—would agree young people today fit the description well. The statistics backing up that assertion are legion: anxiety, depression, family dysfunction, fatherlessness, gender confusion, panic attacks, substance abuse, suicide, and more. And the statistical trends seem headed in the wrong direction. As Astro, my favorite cartoon dog from the iconic 1960s show *The Jetsons* might say at this point: "Ruh-roh!"

While I've seen and been involved in some activities in youth ministry that now make me cringe (and, on occasion, repent), I'm proud of my tribe and our decades of ministry among young people. That said, I do believe it's time for something more radical, invasive, and re-formational than another youth ministry shift. Youth ministry may not be in a crisis of Titanic proportions that will soon sink us, but according to the statistics, we're taking on some serious water.

When the ancient Greek physician Hippocrates remarked, "Desperate times require desperate measures" (*Aphorisms,* 400 BC) He could have been speaking about youth ministry. And I believe we must lead with desperate prayer.

In the cultural moment I'm writing, craziness reigns. (And if you read this book years later, I imagine your own flavor of crazy is going on). In the political realm, national divisiveness and international turmoil keep increasing, exacerbated by social media. We still hotly debate the causes and remedies for rapid climate change. COVID19 waned but many still die from it daily. A once stable and growing economy cratered in the wake of the pandemic, and uncertainty persists as stocks rise and fall wildly. A string of senseless murders set off a firestorm of protests against a culture of racism and white supremacy persisting in the United States far too long.

At a recent gathering of youth workers in Portland to address "Youth Ministry Orthodoxy in a Pluralist Culture," a short list of challenges they face was compiled: sexual identity/LGBTQ issues, pornography, the reality of hell, Christian Nationalism, polyamorous relationships, pornography, abortion, trauma/mental health, masculinity/femininity, premarital sex, and social media. Yikes and yikes again.

While relevant cultural, economic, environmental, medical, or political solutions exist, they're short-term band-aids. Scripture is clear: "If My people, who are called by My name, will humble themselves and pray and seek My face and turn from their wicked ways, then will I hear from heaven and will forgive their sin and will heal their land" (2 Chron. 7:14).

Humble ourselves. Pray. Seek His face. Turn from our wicked ways. These four responses should be embraced by American Christians, Democrat or Republican or whatever, during this season when America's wounds are openly festering. Only God can heal America, and I believe He will if His people respond appropriately.

A Holy Hush

A number of years ago, youth pastors and students corporately glimpsed what a 2 Chronicles 7:14 response looked like. "Prayer in the Square: One Night" featured 4,000 to 5,000 students gathered in Pioneer Courthouse Square in downtown Portland, Oregon for a night of corporate worship and prayer. The evening had few of the usual trappings that accompany a youth rally – just worship and heartfelt prayer.

One part of the evening stood out as unique. During the course of our praying, we asked the crowd to kneel in the Square as a sign of humility, and to repent on behalf of both themselves and the church in general for our failure to consistently live in a way that demonstrates the love of Christ to a world trapped in darkness. We weren't the only folks occupying the Square that night; street kids, the homeless, and many others used it as a gathering place. Early on, hecklers sought to interrupt and disrupt us. The tension in what is called "Portland's living room" was palpable. But when we knelt before God in the midst of our city, the Square suddenly quieted. It was as if a Holy Hush descended on the place; for a few minutes, there was no heckling, no shouting, no commotion around the edges. Just several thousand kids in silence before their God.

A youth pastor wrote to me the next day: "Something quite astounding took place during the corporate kneeling and silent prayer. A position of humility as such displayed a 'one voice' prayer to our Holy Father in a place where holiness is completely unrecognized. It was beautiful." While God hasn't healed Portland (yet–if you follow the news, this is painfully obvious, as of this writing), I do know for a few minutes, heaven came down to earth.

I understand that Old Testament promises such as 2 Chronicles 7:14 made to the nation of Israel don't always directly apply to today's nations and situations. Yet, I am convinced a posture of humility, repentance, and surrender from God's people across our country, both individually and corporately, could bring a significant measure of heaven's healing to our slice of the earth. The same is true for the re-formation of youth ministry.

Victory through Surrender

Another one of my go-to passages is 2 Chronicles 20. To me, these verses wrap humility, repentance and surrender together in one package. When Jehoshaphat, King of Judah, discovered invading armies at his doorstep, his usual response would've been to sound the shofar (bugle) and muster his army as quickly as possible to defend the city. That was the standard operating procedure in a country not unfamiliar with invading armies and warfare tactics. But Jehoshaphat didn't respond per usual. The invading armies loomed too big and too close. He realized that despite the reputation of Judah's army as valiant warriors, this particular battle had defeat written all over it.

So, Jehoshaphat responded by calling his people together, not to prepare for battle, but for prayer and fasting. He led his people in a heart-felt prayer and acknowledged God's sovereignty (vs. 6) and past faithfulness (vs. 7-9). But it is the end of his prayer that revealed his heart. Read it carefully: "O our God, will you not judge them? For we have no power to face this vast army that is attacking us. *We do not know what to do, but our eyes are upon you*" (20:12, *italics mine*).

Jehoshaphat's conclusion revealed some key concepts in his thinking. First, he humbly admitted that Judah, on her own, possessed no chance of victory. On a human plane the king and his warriors couldn't muster enough power to defeat this enemy. Second, he admitted that as a seasoned military commander in charge of veteran troops, he didn't know how to divert disaster. So, he shifted his focus and that of his countrymen not on the battle or opposing armies, but on God and God alone. Their eyes were firmly fixed on the only source of victory and the power to accomplish it.

God responded to Jehoshaphat's humble prayer with a prophetic word of encouragement from the Levite Jahaziel (vs.14-17), as well as a battle strategy unlike any they had utilized before: they were to place at the front of the army not the shield bearers, or spear throwers, or archers, but the worship leaders! (I bet they were pretty excited about that.)

The Chronicler recorded the result: "After consulting the people, Jehoshaphat appointed men to sing to the Lord and to praise Him for the splendor of His holiness as they went out at the head of the army, saying: 'Give thanks to the Lord, for His love endures forever.' As they began to sing and praise, the Lord set ambushes against the men of Ammon and Moab and Mount Seir who were invading Judah, and they were defeated" (20:21-22).

I think Jehoshaphat's example can be foundational in our pursuit of youth ministry re-formation. Jehoshaphat turned to God in humility, repentance, and desperate prayer because he didn't possess another option. As youth workers engaged in an epic spiritual battle for the lives of emerging generations of youth, do we know another option? Do we really think the solution to regaining traction in reaching young people for Christ involves reaching yet again into our seemingly bottomless bag of youth ministry tricks of the trade?

Insanity has been defined as doing the same thing over and over again and expecting different results (usually attributed to Albert Einstein). Youth workers are not insane. They increasingly acknowledge that current strategies and methodologies, while certainly good ones, are insufficient for the task at hand with American youth. While we may or may not be losing the battle for the souls of American youth, we believe God holds much more for us. We believe God wants the Great Commission fulfilled among the emerging generations. But . . . we must change our current approach. To paraphrase author and ministry leader Henry Blackaby, we must discover what is on God's heart so we can join Him in His mission (*Experiencing God,* 1990).

I want to be very careful here not to throw our entire youth ministry enterprise under the bus. I get around enough to see ample evidences of effective, fruitful ministry to youth. That being said, I'm afraid that, far too often, contemporary youth ministry gives in to the Western culture tendency to make great plans, then ask God to bless them, as opposed to ask God for His plans, then respond in faith through obedient action. Perhaps one of the more important things we can do as youth workers is to follow Jehoshaphat's example, and adopt a posture of humility, repentance, and surrender. We can admit "we don't know what to do" to reach the emerging generations. We can fix our eyes on Jesus, await His instructions, and commit to faithful obedience when we hear from Him.

As we do so, I hope we're prepared for what we will hear. Jehoshaphat was likely not thrilled when he was told to put the worship leaders at the front of the army. Nor was Gideon when his army was whittled down from 32,000 to 300 men, with their weapons of choice being empty jars, torches and trumpets. But they both obeyed. And God gave them both victory.

"He who has an ear, let him hear what the Spirit says to the churches" (Rev. 3:6).

Chapter 2

The Holy Youth Worker

But just as he who called you is holy, so be holy in all you do; for it is written: "Be holy, because I am holy."

—1 Peter 1:15-16

THIS IS, TO ME, the most important chapter in the book. I could have called it "Hindrances to Prayer" because this is, after all, a book on prayer, and what follows certainly has a lot to do with hindrances. But I have stuck with what you see above because I am absolutely convinced that desperate, prayer-driven youth ministry re-formation must begin with the ultimate prayer prerequisite: personal holiness and purity. So let's start with mine.

My walk with Jesus today is characterized by growing intimacy and obedience, but this hasn't always been the case. In the past, too often I tolerated secret sins while maintaining a public veneer of righteousness. I've engaged with other youth workers—including mentors who should have known better—in behavior that was highly questionable, if not outright sinful. I frankly, have seen, heard, and tolerated conduct at youth worker gatherings, event green rooms, and conference penthouses that shame me today. Over the years, more than a few of my youth ministry mentors and peers have morally or ethically imploded in public ways. On behalf of myself and my generation of youth ministry leaders, I repent.

An Honest Assessment

I write the following words with fear and trembling because I don't want to be misunderstood. What I have learned through my own lengthy struggles is that the key to effective personal prayer isn't passion or persistence or perseverance. Those are all important and I will touch on them in the rest of the book. But I believe the key to intimacy with the Father and a vibrant prayer life depends on personal holiness and purity. And here is where the fear and trembling kick in: my ministry experience over the decades reveals that personal holiness and purity might not be one of our greatest strengths as youth workers.

I know many youth workers who keep short accounts with God. I could provide a lengthy list (many likely familiar to you) of men and women of God who work with youth and from what I can tell, are a pure as the driven snow. I'm not the chief of the purity police—far from it, considering my battles in this area—and I won't judge the hearts of brothers and sisters I love so dearly. But is there a connection between the lack of power in our prayers and the purity of our hearts? As we seek to mentor kids in the arena of prayer, do we fail to place enough emphasis on the importance of personal holiness? I think so.

Personal Holiness Unpacked

While some of the people I looked up to in my early years of youth ministry had moral and/or sexual failures, it's not biblically accurate to limit our definition of holiness to those two categories, as important as they are. Let me elaborate.

After David finally assumed his throne King of Israel and captured Jerusalem, he was desperate to transport the Ark of the Covenant to the place he was establishing as the capital city of Israel. But he didn't just want the Ark there as an artifact from the days of Moses. He wanted what dwelled in between the cherubim on the top of the Ark: the Presence of God. He wanted God's Presence as close as possible, for him personally and for his nation. So, he assembled a small contingent—30,000 chosen men—and headed to Abinadab's shack to fetch it. That is where the Ark had resided since the Philistines, who captured it years previously and subsequently saw their cities of Ashdod and Ekron devastated (see 1 Samuel 4-5), had freaked out and returned it in a hurry (1 Sam. 6:1-7:1).

Fetching the ark was a good idea. What was not a good idea was transporting it on a cart rather than the method prescribed by God, which was by poles run through the rings on the side of the ark, and carried on the shoulders of Levites. You know what happened—the cart tipped, Abinadab's son, Uzzah, reached out to steady the ark, and it cost him his life. A chastened David left the Ark at Obed-Edom's place for three months and as a result, God richly blessed this household.

Eventually, David regrouped for another try. This time he did it right, maybe even to the point of overkill. The text says, "When those who were carrying the Ark of the LORD had taken six steps, [David] sacrificed a bull and a fattened calf" (2 Sam. 6:13). If that happened every six steps throughout the journey, then they would have sacrificed nearly 3,000 bulls and 3,000 calves along the way!

A parallel account appears in 1 Chronicles, where we also discover a fascinating explanation by David of his original blunder: "It was because you, the Levites, did not bring it up the first time that the Lord our God broke out in anger against us. We did not inquire of him about how to do it in the prescribed way" (15:13). God isn't satisfied with us making assumptions about how He would like things done. He likes to be asked.

David learned that purity and holiness is really, really important to God, even when it doesn't seem all that vital. After all, wasn't the act of bringing the ark to Jerusalem much more important than the manner it transported? Apparently not. David later penned

Psalm 24, about meeting God's requirements. The first two verses
create a prelude, focusing on God as Creator; the last four focus on
the arrival of God as King of Glory at His sanctuary. The middle
four verses focus on God as Holy, specifying the qualifications one
must possess to have access to Him: "Who may ascend the hill of
the LORD? Who may stand in his holy place? He who has clean
hands and a pure heart, who does not lift up his soul to an idol or
swear by what is false. He will receive blessing from the LORD and
vindication from God his Savior. Such is the generation of those
who seek him, who seek your face, O God of Jacob" (vs. 3-6).

The qualifications for those who may "ascend" and "stand"
are clear:

Clean hands: purity of actions.
Pure heart: purity of attitudes and motives.
Does not lift up his soul to an idol: purity of worship.
Or swear by what is false: purity of truth-telling.

That's a whole lot of purity! Psalm 15, similar thematically to
the central portion of Psalm 24, adds a number of qualifications
to dwell in God's sanctuary and live on His holy hill. The entire
purity list can be rather intimidating! Especially when you throw in
New Testament passages regarding characteristics of holy living. For
example, Ephesians 4:17—5:21. But here is Psalm 15:

LORD, who may dwell in your sacred tent?
    Who may live on your holy mountain?
The one whose walk is blameless,
    who does what is righteous,
    who speaks the truth from their heart;
whose tongue utters no slander,
    who does no wrong to a neighbor,
    and casts no slur on others;

who despises a vile person
    but honors those who fear the LORD;
who keeps an oath even when it hurts,
    and does not change their mind;
who lends money to the poor without interest;
    who does not accept a bribe against the innocent.
Whoever does these things
    will never be shaken.

What is clear from these two Psalms is that David served—and we serve—a holy God who determines our access to Him according to our personal holiness and purity. Then and now, it's impossible to attain, or maintain, that level of purity. It was (and is) the sacrifice of the high priest alone—in our case, Christ (Heb. 7:27-28)—that provides access to God (1 Jn. 1:7, 9). Christ's finished work on the Cross provides for our positional holiness. Yet, God still expected a trajectory towards practical purity in the life of David, and He expects the same in our lives today—not perfection, but what the theologians call progressive sanctification, defined as "the ongoing work of God's grace whereby He enables believers to put sin to death in their lives and conforms them more and more to the image of Christ" (www.ligonier.org/guides/sanctification).

Obedience, Blessings, Answered Prayer

If you take a close look at John 13 through 17, you will notice that the words "holy" and "purity" are not mentioned. However, Jesus took great pains to ensure His followers understood the connection between obedience—holiness and purity in action—and answered prayer. He said:

> "I tell you the truth, anyone who has faith in me will do what I have been doing. He will do even greater things

than these, because I am going to the Father. And I will do whatever you ask in my name, so that the Son may bring glory to the Father. You may ask me for anything in my name, and I will do it." (14:12)

"I am the vine; you are the branches. If a man remains in me and I in him, he will bear much fruit; apart from me you can do nothing . . . If you remain in me and my words remain in you, ask whatever you wish, and it will be given you." (15:5, 7)

"If you obey my commands, you will remain in my love, just as I have obeyed my Father's commands and remain in his love . . . You did not choose me, but I chose you and appointed you to go and bear fruit—fruit that will last. Then the Father will give you whatever you ask in my name." (15:10,16)

"In that day you will no longer ask me anything. I tell you the truth, my Father will give you whatever you ask in my name. Until now you have not asked for anything in my name. Ask and you will receive, and your joy will be complete." (16:23-24)

Jesus' last time with His disciples before the Cross proved significant in many ways. He surely wanted to emphasize the more salient aspects of His teachings over the past few years. For our purposes, one theme stands out: abiding in Christ—obedient living—is a key to both fruitful ministry: "apart from me you can do nothing" (14:12), and answered prayer: "You may ask me for anything in my name, and I will do it" (vs. 12). Later Scripture writers further develop this:

Dear friends, if our hearts do not condemn us, we have confidence before God and receive from Him anything we ask, because we obey His commands and do what pleases Him. (1 Jn. 3:21-22)

You do not have, because you do not ask God. When you ask, you do not receive, because you ask with wrong motives, that you may spend what you get on your pleasures. (Jas. 4:2b-3)

The end of all things is near. Therefore, be clear minded and self-controlled so that you can pray. (1 Pet. 4:7)

And when you stand praying, if you hold anything against anyone, forgive him, so that your Father in heaven may forgive you your sins. (Mk. 11:25)

Pursuing Practical Purity

I'm aware I've covered material that may seem basic for many of us. We know, and teach our kids, that sin quenches the Spirit and hinders our prayer lives, and that confession of that sin restores the connection and access. But if we make a habit of watching R-rated movies or streaming raunchy shows to "better understand the culture," allowing the accompanying filth to infiltrate our minds and hearts, can we expect to upgrade our prayer lives? And while we're on the subject: Internet porn rages among men and women, and the youth we work with, all available with a few clicks of a computer or smartphone. It's also epidemic among youth pastors. We need to aspire to a new standard of purity.

Perhaps more often than not, the purity issue in our hearts isn't overt like porn, but more subtle. Yet, ultimately the more "subtle" purity issues are just as destructive, if not checked. For much of my Christian experience I've struggled with addictive behaviors. The behaviors that entrap me don't appear on the assumed list of no-nos for Christians. These are practices that you may do, or partake of, with no problem at all. But for me, they are Hebrews 12:1 "hindrances." That verse advises: "Therefore, since we are surrounded by such a great cloud of witnesses, let us throw off everything that hinders and the sin that so easily entangles. And let us run with perseverance the race marked out for us. . . ."

The verse distinguishes between "everything that hinders," and "the sin that so easily entangles us." The latter aren't stated sins, but problems, nonetheless. Both inhibit our ability to "run with perseverance the race marked out for us." From time to time the Holy Spirit shows me something that is, for me, a hindrance. James 4:17 says, "Anyone, then, who knows the good he ought to do and doesn't do it, sins." It may not be sin for you, but it's sin for me. If I don't deal with it, my purity gets compromised and, accordingly, so is my prayer life.

A Welsh Example

"Over one hundred years ago, a college student in Wales named Evan Roberts, aged twenty-six, obtained permission to leave college to return to his home village of Lougher to preach his first sermon. Seventeen people showed up to listen to his four points . . . three months later a hundred thousand converts had been added to the churches of Wales" (*Campus Aflame*, Regal, 1971). Ideally, I want to respond like Roberts, a catalyst to the Welsh Revival in the early 1900s. When asked about the personal prerequisites to an outpouring of the Spirit, he offered these four points:

Confess all known sin.
Put away all doubtful things and forgive everyone.
Obey the promptings of the Holy Spirit.

Publicly confess Christ as your Savior. (DeMoss and
Grisson, *Seeking Him: Experiencing the Joy of Personal
Revival*, Moody 2009)

Yet, truth be told, part of me sometimes responded with justifica-
tions when confronted by the Spirit about addictive behaviors. I ratio-
nalized most of them. And I could use up a good amount of writing
real estate right now doing so, so you might think better of me.

I've been around more than a few spiritual giants and world-
class intercessors who need their cup of java to get going in the
morning. It's not a problem for them, but it became so for me
when I started consuming copious amounts of hyper-caffeinated
tea get me through my one-and-a-half-hour commute to seminary,
and then I couldn't stop. I then moved to soft drinks, then chewing
tobacco—both stimulants. (Thankfully, I hate the taste of coffee!)

There is an oft-quoted anecdote regarding evangelist Dwight
L. Moody visiting England to meet Charles Spurgeon. Upon
knocking on his door, Spurgeon appeared with a lit cigar in his
hand. Moody exclaimed, "How could you, a man of God, smoke
that cigar?" Spurgeon then pointed at Moody's protruding belly
and said, "The same way that you, a man of God, can be that fat." I
know youth workers who enjoy more than the occasional cigar, but
nicotine is dangerously addictive to me. It took me a long time to
shake that chewing tobacco addiction.

Alcohol, cigars, food, soft drinks, tea, and numerous other
actions and activities can be permissible if they pass biblical muster,
but not if they master us. Scripture says this:

"I have the right to do anything," you say—but not everything is beneficial. (1 Cor. 6:12)

"I have the right to do anything"—but not everything is
constructive. (1 Cor. 10:23)

To the pure, all things are pure, but to those who are corrupted and do not believe, nothing is pure. In fact, both their minds and consciences are corrupted. (Tit. 1:15)

Often, the only way to know what is permissible for us is to ask the Holy Spirit. He'll point out negative influences, be it an entangling sin like Internet porn, or a hindrance like an addiction to social media, politics, shopping, sports talk radio, television/ cable/streaming shows, the stock market, or anything else with the potential to distract us and compromise our purity. If you are really, truly desirous of an upgraded prayer life, now might be a good time to ask Him: "Search me, O God, and know my heart; test me and know my anxious thoughts. See if there is any offensive way in me, and lead me in the way everlasting" (Ps.139:23-24).

Life Soundtracks

David Crosby, one of the founding members of the group Crosby, Stills, and Nash (and sometimes Young) passed away during the early stages of writing this book. I found CSN songs involuntarily playing in my mind over the next several days, like a background life soundtrack. Upon reflection, that made sense. Their music was among my favorites during my teenage years. The whole life soundtrack thing got me feeling a bit nostalgic, so I compiled a list of artists who influenced me through their music from my early teens to the present.

In order, my life soundtrack consists of: The Beach Boys; The Beatles; The Dave Clark Five; Cream; Blind Faith; Crosby, Stills, and Nash; Neil Young; James Taylor; Joni Mitchell; America; Randy Stonehill; 2nd Chapter of Acts; Keith Green; John Fahey; John Prine; Gordon Lightfoot; David Wilcox; Kelly Jo Phelps; Delirious?; Misty Edwards; Sandra McCracken; and Indelible Grace. (not included on this list, but my favorite band name ever: Plankeye.)

While most of us have life soundtracks—various songs that tend to play in the back of our minds while doing life—I have found that we can curate our life soundtracks. What we listen to most ends up on in our soundtrack, and as followers of Christ we should be compelled to be intentional in our soundtrack curation, choosing to listen—not exclusively, but primarily—to music that fits biblical parameters:

Finally, brothers, whatever is true, whatever is noble, whatever is right, whatever is pure, whatever is lovely, whatever is admirable—if anything is excellent or praiseworthy—think about such things. (Phil. 4:8)

Speak to one another with psalms, hymns and spiritual songs. Sing and make music in your heart to the Lord. (Eph. 5:19)

Let the word of Christ dwell in you richly as you teach and admonish one another with all wisdom, and as you sing psalms, hymns and spiritual songs with gratitude in your hearts to God. (Col. 3:16)

Yes, I have a Mike's Greatest Hits playlist, containing music from most of the musicians listed above that I listen to from time to time. But in general, I've grown more careful and prayerful about what I turn loose to play in my head. A life soundtrack does make a difference in my walk with Jesus. Am I nitpicking regarding music? Let Scripture and the Holy Spirit make the final call on that.

Forgiveness

One more thing about David Crosby and CSN(Y) that has to do with personal holiness and purity. Once upon a time I owned vinyl albums produced by many of the artists on my life soundtrack music list. Today we own a turntable and could play those albums if I still had my collection. But I got rid of those albums long ago, mostly because I took such poor care of them that scratches rendered them almost unplayable. Similarly, the legacy of CSN for me got "scratched up" because of the group's apparent bitterness and unforgiveness. After the halcyon days of the 1960s and 70s the group recorded and toured only sporadically. They formally broke up in 2016, mostly because of internal disputes that ended up going public in some nasty ways. I hoped they would reconcile and reunite so I could hear those remarkable harmonies one more time, maybe even see them in concert. Now that will never happen.

Radio personality Howard Stern understood this when he said to David Crosby in an SiriusXM interview: "What I worry about, as we all approach the end of our lives here, as we get older, it would be really sad if one of you went and there wasn't some sort of reconciliation" (www.youtube.com/watch?v=JqjoEkOg-Bo).

In a similar vein, *The Guardian* journalist Simon Hatterstone concluded a lengthy 2022 written interview with Graham Nash as follows: "Suddenly the mood has changed. I stare at him, trying to work out what he is thinking. I seem to be looking at a man with the implacable resolve to follow his heart and live his rock'n'roll life to the last. But I also seem to be witnessing the desperate melancholy of an elderly man aware of all he has lost" (www.theguardian.com/music/2022/may/03/graham-nash).

No matter the soundtrack of your life, unforgiveness will scratch it so badly that the music will be unrecognizable. It's impossible to live a holy, pure life with unforgiveness present. When Jesus modeled how to pray, He included: "Forgive us our debts, as we all have forgiven our debtors" (Mt. 6:9-13). He then elaborated: "For if you forgive men when they sin against you, your heavenly Father will forgive you. But if you do not forgive men their sins, your Father will not forgive your sins" (vs. 14-15).

In case that doesn't get our attention, we have Jesus cursing a fig tree, which at the time made little sense to His followers. But Mark the gospel writer recorded how Jesus used the withered fig tree as an example of the role of faith and belief in answered prayer. And, in the same breath, the importance of forgiveness:

> "Have faith in God," Jesus answered. "I tell you the truth, if anyone says to this mountain, 'Go, throw yourself into the sea,' and does not doubt in his heart but believes that what he says will happen, it will be done for him. Therefore, I tell you, whatever you ask for in prayer, believe that you have received it, and it will be yours. And when you stand praying, if you hold anything against anyone, forgive him, so that your Father in heaven may forgive you your sins." (Mk. 11:22-26)

Unforgiveness is a big deal to God; and it should be to us, too.

The Bottom Line

"'Everything is permissible'—but not everything is beneficial. 'Everything is permissible'—but not everything is constructive. Nobody should seek his own good, but the good of others" (1 Cor. 10:23-24).

I realize that some readers might consider some of this chapter to be nitpicking, or perhaps smacking of legalism. Point taken; but when it comes to personal holiness and purity, on which side do we want to error? I wonder what would happen if our tribe of youth workers gave a little less focus on the "permissibility" of their behaviors, and a little more focus on the "beneficial" and "constructive" aspects of personal holiness and purity? How about we find out together.

Chapter 3

Resting and Connecting with God

You have made us for yourself, O Lord, and our heart is restless until it rests in You.

—Saint Augustine

The last chapter emphasized the correlation between personal holiness, purity, and effective prayer. If we want to grow in prayer, and teach students to do likewise, we need to take holiness and purity seriously. I know my own lack of holiness hindered my prayers. But it wasn't the only hindrance.

I convene a monthly gathering of secular nonprofit executives in my community, and at a recent meeting the conversation turned to the epidemic of anxiety, depression, panic attacks, and suicide ideations among local teenagers. For those who work with teenagers, this isn't news. It's a grim reality we deal with almost daily. Although this book isn't specifically about mental and spiritual health, this chapter centers on helping teens and us connect and rest with God through prayer. And because these four issues above can hinder prayer, we need to address them. I wish I had a long time ago.

Down In Flames

My transition from local church youth pastor to nonprofit ministry leader was not planned, or smooth. Fifteen years and three churches into my youth pastor career, I woke up after a standard-issue citywide New Year's Eve bash and found myself in a state of profound, paralyzing depression. I had never been depressed before, so it took me a few days to get my bearings. Then after several subsequent months of riding an emotional roller coaster, spending more than a few hours in the offices of a medical doctor and a psychiatrist, and trying in vain to create a "new normal" that allowed me to do my job, I resigned my youth pastorate.

A few weeks later, I stood on the banks of the Deschutes River in Central Oregon with two close friends. They didn't know what to make of my predicament, but thought flyfishing might help. During an afternoon break, I picked up a devotional book one guy brought along and read this: "The Bible everywhere teaches that God is underwhelmed by our best efforts and unimpressed with our most spectacular achievements. *It's not what we do for Him that matters nor should it matter much to us. What matters most is who we are to Him"* (*A Burden Shared,* Discovery House, 1991, *Italics mine*).

The author, David Roper, was unpacking Luke 10:17-20, in which 72 of Jesus' disciples returned from a short-term missions trip elated with their successes. Jesus was elated, too, but also cautioned them: "Do not rejoice that the spirits submit to you, but rejoice that your names are written in heaven." Roper commented, "The disciples felt good about themselves because they had done well. It was far better, Jesus observed, to get one's joy from the knowledge that we are special to God, that He knows our names and has them in His book!" (p. 12).

That brief encounter with Luke 10 and Roper's comments were life-changing for me. I realized I had been basing my identity on my abilities as a youth pastor, subconsciously trying to earn favor with God (as if that was possible) through my ministry prowess, rather than resting in the fact that He loved me, as the old hymn goes, just as I am. Three church splits and life-threatening family illnesses had served to bring this core issue to the surface. From that point on, everything changed for me, including my prayer life, as the truth that God is more concerned about who I am to Him than what I do for Him (as if He, really, needs me to do anything for Him) settled in my soul.

A Formula for Wellness

In the years since that trauma, I've practiced a formula that isn't original with me and may seem overly simplistic, but describes my own healing journey:

Identity + purpose + belonging = meaning = *shalom* (peace)

Since my season with depression, I have been on a steady learning curve, moving from identity to shalom. As my identity has become increasingly rooted in Christ and who the Bible says I am (Col. 2:6-7) rather than taking my cues from the culture or social media or any other source; as my purpose in life (2 Cor. 5:9) become increasingly clear; and as I have discovered that I belong to the family of God and need to be regularly connected to the body of Christ, my life has taken on a new, biblically rooted meaning. I have found shalom, peace and rest for my soul.

My soul finds rest in God alone; my salvation comes from him. He alone is my rock and my salvation; he is my fortress; I will never be shaken. (Ps. 62:1-2)

"Take my yoke upon you and learn from me, for I am gentle and humble in heart, and you will find rest for your souls." (Mt. 11:29)

The Lord replied, "My Presence will go with you, and I will give you rest." (Ex. 33:14)

As my wife, Terri, would tell you, while I get rest at night, a posture of being "at rest" is something I've been slow to acquire. She's dealt with a litany of my nervous habits. It's hard for me to sit still. I don't have nervous tics, per se, but being at rest has not been my strength. My history is one of a "human doing" rather than a "human being." I've tended to make great plans, then ask God to bless them, rather that asking God for the plans, waiting for Him to respond, and carrying them out in obedience. Thankfully, Terri would also tell you I've improved in these areas. And that my praying has correspondingly improved.

The biblical word for "rest" is closely aligned to the Hebrew word shalom. While the primary meaning of shalom is "peace," it can also mean harmony, wholeness, completeness, prosperity, welfare and tranquility. All of which can be summed up in one phrase: human flourishing, the way God intended. The more I am at rest and shalom, the better I can pray. The more we help kids discover their true identity, purpose, and belonging, the more they will rest, the deeper they will connect with God, and the better they will pray.

I'm aware I've presented a rather simplistic overview here; my daughter works as a seminary-trained therapist who deals with this stuff on a daily basis, and would agree with my assessment. But she and I would also agree: there aren't enough counselors and therapists and medications in the world to deal with the explosion of anxiety, depression, panic attacks, and suicidal ideations among teens . . . and parents . . . and people in vocational ministry.

Puppy at Rest

In the midst of working on this chapter, I went downstairs for a lunch break. We live on a river, in the mountains, with one year-around neighbor within five miles. Our home also serves as a private retreat house, where people arrive to get help and get better. The setting is ideal for that.

As I write, we have four feet of snow in the yard and it is nasty cold outside. But that doesn't stop our neighbor's dog, a Kuvasz, from blazing a trail to our place. She spends more time here than at her owner's house because he treats her like the sheep dog she is, while we approach her like a beloved pet and smother her with attention. When I arrived downstairs, Terri pointed to a glass door where Puppy (our name for this huge dog) basked in the sun on our deck. She saw us watching her, and while her tail beat wildly against the deck, she didn't move in our direction. She was at rest, experiencing "doggy shalom" if there is such a thing.

We can learn many methods, tips, and techniques regarding prayer, and I'll discuss them in the next chapters, along with ways to impart those things to youth groups. But all of that is no substitute for rest for our souls, found in God alone. Shalom is, along with holiness and purity, the foundation for connecting with God and developing a corresponding healthy prayer life.

"The LORD bless you and keep you; the LORD make His face shine on you and be gracious to you; the LORD turn His face toward you and give you peace." (Num. 6:24-26)

"Come to me, all you who are weary and burdened, and I will give you rest. Take my yoke upon you and learn from me, for I am gentle and humble in heart, and you will find rest for your souls. For my yoke is easy and my burden is light." (Matt. 11:28-30)

My soul finds rest in God alone;
my salvation comes from him.
He alone is my rock and my salvation;
he is my fortress, I will never be shaken. (Ps. 62:1-2)

SELAH

Quantum Jesus: Paradoxology Prayer

For by Him all things were created: things in heaven and on earth, visible and invisible, whether thrones or powers or rulers or authorities; all things were created by Him and for Him. He is before all things, and in Him all things hold together.

—Col. 1:16-17

(NOTE: THE WORD "SELAH" is found 71 times in the Psalms and three times in Habakkuk, of all places. Scholars aren't quite sure what it means. Some think it to be a pause in the text, while others think it is some kind of musical term. I'm treating it here, and one more time later in the book, as a pause. What follows could be taken, at first glance, as a departure from my prayer theme. In my opinion, that is not at all the case, which is why I am including it. And feel free, if you think selah is a musical term, to hum along as you read.)

I've long been fascinated by Quantum Physics, the study of matter and energy at a fundamental level. Although to be clear, there is a vast difference between fascination and understanding;

while I am strong in the former, I am also quite lame in the latter. A half-dozen books on various aspects of the topic are in my library. My former favorite movie of all time, *2001: A Space Odyssey* (for which I have been mocked by my wife and children for decades) has been replaced by *Interstellar*, another space movie in which Quantum Physics plays a huge role.

And, of course, there is the Higgs Boson (also known as the "God Particle"), the discovery of which led to very-distant relative Peter Higgs and a colleague receiving a Nobel Prize in physics. What is the Higgs Boson? Uh . . . it is a sub-atomic particle, existing within the universe-wide Higgs Field, that gives all other particles (except photons) mass or weight. An illustration may help: if you pass an object through a body of water, it will emerge wet because it picks up some of the water. Similarly (kind of), the particles that make up our universe pick up Higgs Bosons because the Higgs Field fills the entire universe. Uncle Peter predicted the existence of said boson, and in a 2012 experiment at the Large Hadron Collider (located 573 feet beneath the France-Switzerland border), scientists smashed protons into each other at near the speed of light, and the resulting wreckage included the Higgs Boson. They think.

If that makes your brain ache, hang on . . . according to Quantum Physics (also known as Quantum *Mechanics* or *Theory*): Everything in the material universe (that we can observe and measure) consists of "packets" (or "quanta," hence the name) of energy that exhibit behaviors of both waves and particles, continually vibrate at various frequencies, can exist in more than one place at one time, and can move from one place to another at faster than the speed of light. Particles that have picked up Higgs Bosons have weight; particles that don't are photons, and make up electromagnetic radiation (think radio waves, microwaves, infrared waves, ultraviolet waves, x rays, gamma rays, visible light, and so on.) that permeates the entire universe—literally, everywhere . . . and then there is dark matter . . . and dark energy . . . which is the stuff scientists can't observe and measure, but think is there.

Quantum Spirituality

Whoa! Wait a minute, you were expecting more stuff on prayer, not a *Quantum Physics for Dummies* primer, right? Be patient, we'll get there, but in the meantime . . . in the midst of the intellectual challenges and just plain weirdness that is Quantum Physics, there is some spiritually encouraging, exciting and relevant stuff. One of the best examples: if the universe is comprised entirely of packets or quanta, of energy, with the ones picking up Higgs bosons becoming matter with mass, and the others becoming electromagnetic radiation . . . what if the biblical injunction, "Let there be light" (Genesis 1:3) is a description of God creating and filling the universe with not just visible light (which is only *visible* to us because our eyes are made to pick up this very narrow frequency of electromagnetic radiation) but *light* defined more broadly as quantum energy packets? It would be as if God, "in the beginning," filled His newly created universe with material from which He would fashion the galaxies, the stars, the earth and sun, and all the rest of what is found in the Genesis account—including the men and women created in His image. I'm sorry, but is that cool or what?! Some further examples:

- Quantum Physics is making it increasingly clear that the material universe in which we exist does **not** operate in the ways that scientists and naturalists have long assumed it does. There is increasing evidence of a unifying, grand design; Something seems to be holding everything together. ". . . and in Him all things hold together" (Col. 1:17).
- Quantum Physics turns our rational understanding of time and space on its ear, and helps make the idea of a transcendent God, not bound or limited by time or space, more viable.

- Quanta particles do not always behave in alignment with known laws of physics, thus making them more of a series of probabilities, rather than something that can be scientifically defined and observed. So, everything that we can *see* in the universe is made up of things that we *cannot see*—unseen particles. Which sounds a whole lot like Hebrews 11:3: "By faith we understand that the universe was formed at God's command, so that what is seen was not made out of what was visible."

- Max Planck, winner of a Nobel Prize in Physics and one of the originators of Quantum Theory, famously said: "As a man who has devoted his whole life to the most clear-headed science, to the study of matter, I can tell you as a result of my research about atoms this much: There is no matter as such. All matter originates and exists only by virtue of a force; we must assume behind this force the existence of a conscious and intelligent mind. This mind is the matrix of all matter." (*The New Science*, Meridian Books, 1959)

- Many of the pioneers of Quantum Theory were deists or Christians, and saw their discoveries as illuminating God's methods rather than disproving His existence. One example is John Polkinghorne, a devout Christian and one of the scientists responsible for discovering quarks, a critical part of the quantum model. He retired after 25 years teaching at Cambridge in order to become an Anglican priest.

Without question, much if not all of Quantum Physics is rather out there. But for those so inclined, it can present creative opportunities to direct conversations towards the God who created all things (including Higgs Bosons!) for His purposes and glory, and reveals Himself in the time and space of history through His Son . . . who during His earthly life was, literally, Quantum Jesus.

Theology is, by definition, the study of the nature of God and of belief. Adding flavor and focus to this definition, Roger E. Olson asserts, "Theology is the church's reflection on the salvation brought by Christ and on the gospel of that salvation proclaimed and explained by the First Century apostles" (*The Story of Christian Theology*. IV Press, 1999; pg. 25). People who give attention to this kind of stuff are called theologians, and systematic theology is the attempt of man (and many have done so) to organize these studies into coherent categories.

A Fool's Errand?

Is theology a fool's errand? Yes and no. (I just heard the sound of many books closing. And a few thumping against the wall. Hang in there with me.) Theologies, systematic and otherwise, have been invaluable in helping both clergy and laity better understand what Puritan theologian Stephen Charnock called "the existence and attributes of God." Yet the very nature and attributes to which we rightly assign to God make it difficult, and ultimately impossible, to wrap our finite minds around an infinite God. He is incomprehensible and transcendent (outside of our experience, perception or grasp) yet immanent and (to an extent) knowable: "Now this is eternal life: that they may know you, the only true God, and Jesus Christ, whom you have sent" (Jn. 17:3). He is omniscient (all knowing), omnipresent (present everywhere), omnipotent (all powerful) and a bunch of other fancy words. He has always existed and always will exist. And just this small, meager summary of who God is and what He is like can make one's cranium ache something fierce.

Now, let's apply some of our rudimentary understanding of God to prayer. If God is sovereign, why is prayer necessary? Does God always answer prayer? Can we change God's mind or will by our praying? Why does God sometimes (or often) seem distant or even absent when we are praying? At any one moment, there are probably millions of people praying. How does God hear them all and give them all adequate attention? And how does prayer *really* work, anyway?

In an earlier book, *Youth Ministry On Your Knees*, I attempted to answer many of these questions. And I think I did an OK job of doing so. But almost 20 years later, I realize that my answers, while helpful, were somewhat insufficient. They did not make room for the *mysteries* of prayer.

When it comes to our understanding of prayer (and of God), I think the best posture to take is similar to that of many (most, if they are honest) quantum physicists. The late pioneering quantum physicist and Nobel Laureate Richard Feynman sums it up well: "If you think you understand quantum mechanics, then you don't . . . I think I can safely say that nobody understands quantum mechanics" (*The Character of Physical Law*. MIT Press, 1995).

> "'For my thoughts are not your thoughts, neither are your ways my ways,' declares the Lord. 'As the heavens are higher than the earth, so are my ways higher than your ways and my thoughts than your thoughts.'" (Is. 55:8-9)

In 1 Cor. 4:1, Paul gives us some counsel as we seek to make the inexplicable at least somewhat explainable: "Let a man so account of us, as of the ministers of Christ, and stewards of the mysteries of God." (KJV) This verse is crazy rich in content. The word *"ministers"* actually has a literal meaning of "under-rowers." Picture a movie featuring an ancient sailing ship that, when the winds are unfavorable, is propelled by scores of oarsmen rowing below the deck. The oarsmen cannot see where they are going; they just take orders from the master who is up on the deck. And *stewards* are, literally, those with the responsibility of distributing from a storehouse. So, we are under-rowers of Christ, taking our orders from the Master because He knows "where we are going," and at the same we bear the responsibility of disseminating the "mysteries of God," to those under our care. And the mysteries of God, as we have just seen, are many. So, we execute our stewardship with care, with direction from Above, and with an understanding that sometimes our prayer is a Paradoxology: we don't, really, understand God and His ways, but we do so enough to trust Him without reservation: "Now faith is being sure of what we hope for and certain of what we do not see" (Heb. 11:1).

PART TWO

The Upper Room of Daniel: Personal Prayer

THE LIFE OF Daniel has been the subject of many books and inspirational messages, and rightly so. During the season I spoke to youth at retreats and camps, Daniel stepped forward as one of my go-to series. His life taught important principles to youth thousands of years later.

Taken from Jerusalem into captivity as a young man, the royal court groomed Daniel for three years to serve the Babylonian king Nebuchadnezzar. During Daniel's lifetime, he served at least four kings and three kingdoms over a period of 70 years. It's hard to overstate his influence. His resolute and resilient faith in God, while living and working in a radically pagan culture, resulted in him being given great favor and influence. Even the pagan kings acknowledged this:

> "Surely your God is the God of gods and the Lord of kings and a revealer of mysteries. . . . Now I, Nebuchadnezzar, praise and exalt the glorify the King of Heaven." (2:27; 4:37)
>
> Then King Darius wrote to all peoples . . . "I issue a decree that in every part of my kingdom people must fear

and reverence the God of Daniel. For he is the living God
and he endures forever; his kingdom will not be destroyed,
his dominion will never end. He rescues and he saves; he
performs signs and wonders in the heavens and on the
earth." (6:25-27)

While prayer is implied through the first six biographical
chapters of Daniel (and more overtly in the wild prophetic
chapters that follow) it's chapter 6 where we discover the secret of
Daniel's influence. Now serving yet another king, Darius, as one
of the top administrators in his kingdom, Daniel provoked the
jealousy of the administrators and satraps. So they set him up by
convincing the king to issue a decree: pray to Darius only, or off to
the lion's den you go.

Here's Daniel's response: "Now when Daniel learned that the
decree had been published, he went home to his upstairs room
where the windows opened toward Jerusalem. Three times a day he
got down on his knees and prayed, giving thanks to his God, just
as he had done before. Then these men went as a group and found
Daniel praying and asking God for help" (6:10-11).

Most of us know how the story ends: the king unwillingly
threw Daniel's into the lion's den, and the guy emerged the next
morning without a scratch (vs. 13-23). But let's not miss Daniel's
secret: the practice of personal prayer in his upper room.

Personal prayer practice wasn't unusual among Jews. Daniel
didn't open the window so his praying could be on public display,
but rather, because Jews often prayed facing Jerusalem, following
the example in Solomon's prayer: "Hear the supplication of your
servant and of your people Israel when they pray toward this
place. Hear from heaven, your dwelling place, and when you hear,
forgive" (1 Kgs. 8:30).

Similarly, Jews of that time followed David's pattern of
prayer three times a day: "Evening, morning, and noon I cry

out in distress, and he hears my voice" (Ps. 55:17). Even today, Orthodox Jews often practice daily prayer three times: morning prayer (*shacharit*), afternoon prayer (*minchah*), and evening prayer (*arvith* or *maariv*). Regardless, the point isn't the particulars of Daniel's personal practice, but that prayer was so important to him that he was unwilling to compromise his convictions. He demonstrated this character quality back in chapter 1 when he "resolved not to defile himself with the royal food and wine" (vs. 8) while in training as a teenager for service to Nebuchadnezzar.

The following chapters cover personal prayer from different angles, hopefully in ways to enhance your own prayer life and give you tools to help students—and perhaps even their parents—grow in personal prayer. But as much as any spiritual discipline, prayer is "caught" more than taught. In another words, if as a youth worker you're a man or woman of prayer, those around you will notice and "catch" it.

Chapter 4

Finding Your Own Prayer Rhythm

This is the only way we shall ever learn to pray, by just beginning to do it. And as the babbling child learns the art of speech by speaking, and the lark mounts up to the heights of the sky by beating its little wings again and again upon the air, so prayer will teach us how to pray; and the more we pray, the more shall we learn the mysteries, and heights, and depths of prayer.

—A. B. SIMPSON

The great people of the earth today are the people who pray—not those who talk about prayer; nor those who say they believe in prayer; nor those who can explain about prayer; but those who take time to pray.

—S. D. GORDON

I WAS A WET-behind-the-ears leader of a fledgling prayer ministry who somehow found himself at a national prayer consultation in Colorado, and my learning curve was accelerated so quickly that the G-forces were making me dizzy. I was a nobody from nowhere, and one of the few, if any, youth workers in a gathering of hundreds who for the most part led national or international prayer ministries and movements. The wealth of information, inspiration, and impartation was off the charts for me. So, for those three days

I played the human sponge and did my best to absorb everything and anything.

During one session, the leader encouraged participants to form prayer triplets for a time of intercession. Without giving it much thought, I turned my chair around and found myself in a triplet with Evelyn Christenson and Bobbie Byerly. You may not recognize those names, but back in the day, Evelyn led an international prayer ministry, and Bobbie served as the president of Aglow, a national ministry to women. To me, they were the prayer ministry equivalent of sitting down with legendary golfers Jack Nicklaus and Tiger Woods. Or evangelists Billy Graham and Luis Palau. Or basketball greats Lebron James and Steph Curry. Or guitar legends Eric Clapton and Tommy Emmanuel (OK, I got carried away). Now, sitting with these women was intimidating enough, but I was going to have to pray—out loud—with them. Tiger was going to hand me the driver and say, "You tee off first."

To be honest, I have little recollection about how our intercession transpired. I do remember that Evelyn and Bobbie didn't waste brain energy wondering about this guy sitting with them: his identity, or if he could hold his own in united prayer. (I couldn't, but they didn't know that.) They just started praying. I went along for the ride, and learned my first important insight concerning prayer.

Just Do It

Somebody once said, "Ninety percent of success is just showing up." (Who actually said it depends of which online source you use—ha.) This is certainly true when it comes to prayer. Ninety percent of effective praying is just showing up to do it. Eloquence is not the issue— Evelyn and Bobbie prayed with a passion and intimacy unfamiliar to me at the time, but it wasn't like they prayed "Beethoven's Ninth Symphony" while I was praying "Chopsticks." Volume isn't important (God is not hard of hearing) nor does using King James English give one better access to heaven. What is important is that you're doing it; that you just show up and participate, be it in a corporate setting or in your own prayer closet. This was my first insight.

The second insight I learned at that conference is that one of the better ways to grow in prayer is to hang around praying people. A frequently quoted anonymous bit of wisdom says, "Prayer is better caught than taught." After spending decades around world-class prayer warriors, and being married to one, I wholeheartedly concur. That was just as true for me in my infancy in Christ. I accepted Christ as Savior at age 18, and up to that time, my prayer repertoire consisted of grace over meals and a memorized bedtime prayer. I learned early on in my faith journey that "The LORD does not look at the things man looks at. Man looks at the outward appearance, but the LORD looks at the heart" (1 Sam. 16:7). Yet, despite a well-intended heart, I'd no clue how to start praying, what to pray about, how long to pray, how to finish, and so on. And while I certainly learned by reading and studying, I absorbed the most by listening to others pray.

A third truth I have earned about developing my own prayer rhythm is to imitate the prayer life of Jesus. I didn't learn this at the conference; rather, from a book somebody encouraged me to read. *The Imitation of Christ,* written in the early 1400s by the Roman catholic monk Thomas à Kempis (Moody Press Edition, 1981). While this book wasn't primarily about prayer, it led me, indirectly, to a few profound Scriptures:

Be imitators of God, therefore, as dearly loved children and
live a life of love, just as Christ loved us and gave himself up
for us as a fragrant offering and sacrifice to God. (Eph. 5:1-2)

This is how we know we are in him: Whoever claims to live
in him just walk as Jesus did. (1 Jn. 2:6)

Author Margaret Magdalen wrote, "There was obviously something very special about the prayer life of Jesus that led the disciples to say, 'Lord, teach us to pray.' What he taught them and what they have recorded for us of his own practice have been left for us as clues he invites and intends us to pick up, ponder, share and appropriate in our own path of prayer" *(Man of Prayer,* IVP, 1987, p. 15). While a close look at Scriptural clues regarding the prayer life of Jesus is beyond the scope of this book, I'd like to highlight a few I've found especially helpful.

To this day, I am astounded and bewildered that Jesus, the incarnate Son of God, spent an entire night in prayer before choosing His 12 Apostles. Let's be truthful: for most of us, when facing a significant decision, our investment in prayer measures in minutes rather than consecutive hours. I mean, how can you spend multiple hours praying about a single subject or issue without endless repetition or repeated distractions? Yet Luke 6:12-13 records this: "One of those days Jesus went out to a mountainside to pray, and spent the night praying to God. When morning came, he called his disciples to him and chose twelve of them, whom he also designated apostles."

Lonely Places

I've also been challenged by Jesus' preferred choices of prayer location:

> After he had dismissed them, he went up on a mountainside by himself to pray. (Mt. 14:23)

> Very early in the morning, while it was still dark, Jesus got up, left the house and went off to a solitary place, where he prayed. (Mk. 1:35)

> At daybreak Jesus went out to a solitary place. (Lk.4:42)

> But Jesus often withdrew to lonely places and prayed (5:16)

I first learned how to pray in college, when a group would gather on a regular basis at 6:30 a.m. to pray. We prayed in the only "solitary place" we could find, the basement boiler room of our fraternity. More than once, I bowed my head to pray, only to wake up an hour or more later, alone. I wonder if my fraternity brothers would laugh while I snored through their prayers. And my early attempts at withdrawing to a "lonely place" became just that: lonely, with distractions and boredom abounding.

Finding a solitary place these days can be a challenge, especially in an urban setting. But what is even more of a challenge is to find a place in my head where distractions are minimized. Jesus probably recognized that getting to a solitary, lonely place on a regular basis would pose a challenge, which is why He instructed His followers, "But when you pray, go into your room, close the door and pray to your Father, who is unseen" (Mt. 6:6). I get this feeling that if Jesus taught us today, He would add, "And by the way, before you close the door, leave all your screens and electronic devices outside."

Bottom line: the Son of God found it important, even necessary, to make what we would call "extraordinary prayer" a staple in His life, be it praying all night or withdrawing for protracted times of prayer. If He considered that kind of praying essential, how about you and me? Like a muscle that grows through repetitive training, my own prayer life has grown over the years from "seven minutes with God," (a Navigators guide to developing a quiet time) to much more than that. But I'm continually challenged by the example of Jesus to build my prayer endurance muscle even more.

Kaleidoscope Defined

One last important thing I have learned concerning prayer: it's not a one-size-fits-all endeavor. There is a kaleidoscope of ways to go about it. The colored glass in a kaleidoscope changes its design endlessly as you rotate the section containing the loose glass fragments.

Similarly, almost endless options exist when it comes to creating your own prayer rhythm.

Prayer acronyms can be a huge help, such as ACTS (Adoration, Confession, Thanksgiving, Supplication) or AWCIPA (Adoration, Waiting, Confession, Intercession, Petition, Adoration). Pete Greig, the 24-7 Prayer founder developed PRAY (Pause, Rejoice, Ask, Yield), modeled after The Lord's Prayer (*How to Pray. A Simple Guide for Normal People,* NavPress, 2019. While youth workers aren't generally "normal" people, the book is still worth reading.)

You can create an acronym or method that works for you. Prayer journals or diaries can also be helpful when it comes to remembering prayer requests as was as answers to prayer. There have been seasons in my life when prayer lists ruled, and others when my praying was more free form. To re-emphasize an earlier pointy: whatever method(s), tools and resources you employ, success in upgrading your prayer life will be determined to a large extent by the slogan popularized (and quite possibly pirated from Scripture—read John 2:5) by Nike: "Just do it."

Prayer Life Upgrade Steps

In conclusion, one of the better helps I have found for a prayer life upgrade is veteran prayer leader Dick Eastman's "10 Steps to a Practical, Joyful Prayer Life." (*Pray!* Sept./Oct. 2000, p.14.) Below, I've listed His steps with my own comments added.

Find the best possible time and place for prayer. When we built the Oregon home where we raised our family, I designed a window seat in my office as my place of prayer. Now in Idaho there isn't a special seat, but I have a window overlooking wilderness, a river, and the occasional moose or mountain lion. Both have worked well for me.

Forget all previous failures in prayer. Unless I did this, I would be prayer-paralyzed! My failures are legion, but so is my perseverance, so I still seem to be headed in the right direction.

Fight all prayer hindrances fiercely. The more alert we are, the better we can engage in this fight. For me, the best way to deal with a wandering mind is to have a pen and paper handy. When a stray thought or an addition to my to-do list intrudes, I write it down, forget about it, and move on. Prayerwalks (more on this later) are also helpful in staying focused.

Focus on the Lord rather than answers to prayer. The value of a relationship isn't based on what the other person does for us, right?

Follow a meaningful plan of action. Sometimes prayer just happens, but more often than not, it requires a workable plan, as opposed to an unrealistic plan. This might mean incrementally increasing the amount of time you set aside for prayer, or developing and maintaining a prayer list, or scheduling a weekly neighborhood prayerwalk.

Feed on spiritual food every day. Our food is the Word of God. Practically, to transition from feeding on the Word to praying, make prayers of the Bible your own by personalizing them. Many Psalms and prayer passages in Paul's Epistles work well for this.

Fellowship with the Lord in love. Prayer is a continual, developing relationship of mutual love and affection, not solely a duty of discipline.

Forgive every wrong done to you. We covered this in chapter 2; go back if this point is not obvious to you.

Forsake all things that hinder spiritual growth. Again, take a refresher in chapter 2 if necessary.

Finish what you start. Persistence is a key component in acts of prayer. When Jesus' disciples asked Him to teach them to pray, He presented the model of what we call the Lord's Prayer, which was immediately followed by teaching on the importance of persistence. The *NIV* Study Bible notes that in Luke 11:1-13, the word for "boldness" in the text can also be translated "persistence."

When I was in grade school, I would often bounce my leg up and down, while sitting at my desk, probably out of boredom since I had not yet discovered caffeine. One day, I was shocked to discover that after intentionally bouncing my leg for a while, it would continue to bounce without any conscious effort on my part! More than a few decades later (I just tried) it will still do that. My continual practice in grade school developed a life-long habit. Which is what we want prayer to become: a life-long habit. So bounce away!

Chapter 5

Hearing His Voice

Jesus is what God sounds like. He's literally the "living Word of God." Hearing his voice is not so much a skill we must master, therefore, as a master we must meet. All the other ways in the which God communicates—through the Bible, prophecy, dreams, visions, and so on—come through Jesus and point back to him too.

—PETE GREIG

OUR GOD IS a speaking God. He spoke creation into being: "By the word of the LORD were the heavens made, their starry host by the breath of his mouth" (Ps. 33:6). "By faith we understand that the universe was formed at God's command, so that what is seen was not made out of what was visible" (Heb. 11:3). Repeatedly, in Genesis chapter 1 we read, "And God said . . ." Throughout the Old Testament, we see God speaking to His people, either directly or through intermediaries, culminating in Jesus: "In the past God spoke to our forefathers through the prophets at many times and in various ways, but in these last days he has spoken to us by his Son, whom he appointed heir of all things, and through whom he made the universe" (Heb. 1:1-2). While God's intention to communicate to His people rings clear throughout the biblical narrative, Jesus drove the point home. We're all supposed to be able to hear God:

"I tell you the truth, the man who does not enter the
sheep pen by the gate, but climbs in by some other way,
is a thief and a robber. The man who enters by the gate is
the shepherd of his sheep. The watchman opens the gate
for him, and the sheep listen to his voice. He calls his own
sheep by name and leads them out. When he has brought
out all his own, he goes on ahead of them, and his sheep
follow him because they know his voice. But they will
never follow a stranger; in fact, they will run away from
him because they do not recognize a stranger's voice . . .
My sheep listen to My voice; I know them, and they follow
Me." (Jn. 10:1-6, 27)

When it comes to hearing God's voice, it's important to
understand the varied ways God speaks to us. In her "Enliven"
online blog, Helen Calder, a prophetic voice, wrote, "We are using
an earthly expression to express a spiritual concept. You and I use
words, speech, and body language to communicate. However, the
Holy Spirit has many creative ways that He can communicate with
us. We hear God's voice, not with our physical ears, but with our
heart and our spirit" ("Hearing God's Voice," Feb 2014).

Here's an example: my wife hears God's voice clearly and often,
almost daily. It is rarely audible (although I do believe God can
speak to us in an audible voice) but it usually is in thoughts that are
crystal clear in her mind. On the other hand, I rarely hear God's
voice that way. Probably a handful of times each year, I receive
what I call a "download," where I'm literally transcribing what God
impresses upon me. It's not a common occurrence, but for someone who doesn't hear the way his wife does, it's pretty cool. I save
most of these transcriptions in a binder. However, two usual ways
I personally hear God are: (1) impressions on my mind while in
prayer; (2) passages of Scripture the Holy Spirit highlights for me
in unmistakable ways.

De-mystifying the Prophetic

Terri and I also hear God clearly through prophetic voices. Yeah, I know that can be controversial in some circles, and prophetic abuse can be an issue today, as it was in New Testament times. But we aren't "throwing the baby out with the bathwater," nor should you. Scripture is clear: "Do not put out the Spirit's fire; do not treat prophecies with contempt. Test everything. Hold on to the good" (1 Thess. 5:19-21).

We're close friends with a man who has walked with us in life and ministry for 40 years, and it's hard to overstate the accuracy and encouragement of his prophetic words to us. Plus, not long ago, we visited a church where a respected prophetic voice spoke. After the service, the host pastor introduced us to the man. We'd never met him and he knew nothing about us. He proceeded to "read our mail," injecting encouragement into our spirits through facts about us and our ministry he could not have possibly known.

We can all hear God speak: through His Written Word, other believers, sermons and books, nature, prophecies, even dreams. He also speaks to us Spirit to spirit. To be clear, God's voice never contradicts His Written Word. But get this: the transcendent God of the universe wants to speak to each of us—youth worker and teenager—personally, and intimately! As Jesus taught, "He calls His own sheep by name" (Jn. 10:3; see also Heb. 12:22-29; 13:20-21).

Spiritual Ear Wax

Hearing God can be a regular, even normal, experience for all believers. If it's not, spiritual ear wax inhibits our hearing, These might be the reasons, taken from Scripture:

> **Sin** that isn't confessed. We covered this earlier, but it's important enough to repeat:

If I had cherished sin in my heart, the LORD would not
have listened; but God has surely listened and heard
my voice in prayer. (Ps. 66:18-19)

Surely the arm of the LORD is not too short to save,
nor his ear too dull to hear. But your iniquities have
separated you from your God; your sins have
hidden his face from you, so that he will not hear.
(Is. 59:1-2)

See to it that you do not refuse him who speaks. If
they did not escape when they refused him who
warned them on earth, how much less will we, if we
turn away from him who warns us from heaven?
(Heb. 12:25)

Unforgiveness. Again, covered earlier but bears repeating:

"For if you forgive men when they sin against you,
your heavenly Father will also forgive you. But if you
do not forgive men their sins, your Father will not
forgive your sins." (Mt. 6:14-15)

[Jesus said again,] "And when you stand praying, if
you hold anything against anyone, forgive him, so
that your Father in heaven may forgive you your sins."
(Mk. 11:25)

Doubt can also keep us from hearing God clearly.

If any of you lacks wisdom, he should ask God, who
gives generously to all without finding fault, and it will
be given to him. But when he asks, he must believe

and not doubt, because he who doubts is like a wave of the sea, blown and tossed by the wind. That man should not think he will receive anything from the LORD; he is a double-minded man, unstable in all he does. (Jas. 1:5-8)

And without faith it is impossible to please God, because anyone who comes to him must believe that he exists and that he rewards those who earnestly seek him. (Heb.11:6)

Distractions. This deserves a closer look. There are many, many voices demanding our attention—and frequently, our allegiance—these days. It's hard to know even where to begin in listing them. Television used to be toward the top of any list, since not long ago the average American watched four to five hours per day, exposing families to sitcoms, dramas and the like that sometimes covertly, but often overtly, espouse unbiblical values. The news has become less objective and more opinionated; negative or shock-value stories are the norm. Now television has been eclipsed by the ubiquitous screens—computer, smart-phone, tablet, even watch—that gives users instant access the internet (and porn within a few clicks) as well as social media channels. These channels present curated lives, misinformation, and other minutia that feed the addictions of the FOMO (Fear of Missing Out) folks. Political operatives and conspiracy theorists use all these sources, and more, to send their messages into our ears and, they hope, our minds. Then there is advertising, insisting we spend money we don't really have on things we don't really need. The list of voice sources goes on and on and on . . . yikes!

Minimizing and Listening

At our home, we've taken steps to minimize the number and intensity of distracting voices. A screen isn't the focal point of our living room or any other room. Television, broadcast or cable, hasn't been in our household for many years. (If I need to watch the Super Bowl or the final round of The Masters, I can usually find a way to do so). Our Internet arrives via satellite and we use it sparingly. The local newspapers publish once and twice per week, respectively, and stick almost entirely to local news.

No, we didn't build a concrete bunker in the back yard stocked with several years' worth of provisions. And no, we're not cultural, social, and spiritual ostriches with our proverbial heads stuck in the sand. We pay attention to local, state, national, and international news and events. The home pages on our computers include headline feeds from major news sources. Listening is a high priority in our household. We just choose to filter competing voices so our ears stay as attuned as possible to the voice of the Lover of Our Souls.

Ears to the Ground

Addressing the English House of Commons as prime minister in 1941, Winston Churchill remarked, "I heard it said that leaders should keep their ears to the ground. All I can say is that the British nation will find it very hard to look up to the leaders who are detected in that somewhat ungainly posture" (*quoted in Oz Guinness, A Free People's Suicide, pg. 183*).

The prime minister's joking aside, Terri and I understand the importance of "keeping our ears to the ground" to follow trends that help us stay culturally relevant in our work with young people. As intercessors, we understand the value of knowing about happenings and trends around the neighborhood as well as around the world, so as to inform our praying. As citizens, we want to be educated and thoughtful about issues impacting culture and society. I lead a local Chamber of Commerce and I'm expected to be "up to speed" on these things. But we don't want other voices to distract us from hearing the Voice that matters most. Our default position is with our ears pointed up, rather than down.

I was a fan of rock and roll during the 60s and 70s, owned an electric guitar, and both played and listened to this music often, usually very loudly. As a result, I have a bit of trouble distinguishing voices in a crowded, loud room. How much worse, though, if I allow the blaring, demanding voices coming at me from all angles to keep me from distinguishing God's voice!

So, as the voices competing for our attention—and hearts—increase in number and intensity, let's filter them as the Holy Spirit leads, keeping our spiritual ears tuned upward. In the days ahead, cultivating this habit of the heart will become increasing important . . . and fulfilling.

One more thing . . . in helping teenagers learn to pray, it's essential they learn God can and will speak to them! "In the past God spoke to our forefathers through the prophets at many times and in various ways, but in these last days he has spoken to us by his Son" (Heb. 1:1-2). Jesus will speak to them through His Word, circumstances, prophetic words, the wisdom of others, answers to prayer, and importantly, His Holy Spirit to their spirits.

How do they learn? We teach them. How do we do that? We'll get there in a few short chapters.

Chapter 6

Rethinking Spiritual Warfare

*The one concern of the devil is to keep Christians from
praying. He fears nothing from prayerless studies, prayerless
work, and prayerless religion. He laughs at our toil, mocks
at our wisdom, but trembles when we pray.*

—SAMUEL CHADWICK

*How now does Satan hinder prayer? By temptation
to postpone or curtail it by bringing in wandering thoughts
and all sorts of distractions through unbelief
and hopelessness.*

—ANDREW MURRAY

YOUNG LIFE DOES summer camps extremely well. Untold thousands of teenagers have met Christ at one of the 26 camps they operate. One of their newer, and larger facilities is the Washington Family Ranch in eastern Oregon. It consists of three separate camps on 56,000 acres, located pretty much in the middle of nowhere. How did three amazing camps get situated in such a remote location? The answer is a real-life example of Ecclesiastes 2:26: "To the man who pleases him, God gives wisdom, knowledge and happiness, but to the sinner he gives the task of gathering and storing up wealth to hand it over to the one who pleases God."

In 1981, the Bhagwan Shree Rajneesh, leader of a cultish commune outside of Bombay, India, fled to the U.S. with Indian authorities literally chasing him to the airport. Improbably, he ended up establishing Rancho Rajneesh in central Oregon, where he taught a blend of Eastern mysticism mixed with occultism, self-discovery, sexual freedom, and Western materialism. As several ex-followers testified, "He gives you the opportunity to sin like you've never sinned before." On the site of the former Big Muddy Ranch, he broke multiple Oregon land use laws building a self-sustaining community that could hold up to 5,000 residents, complete with an airport, reservoir, all-essential infrastructure, housing, and other structures used for nefarious purposes.

The rise and fall of Rancho Rajneesh is a fascinating story, documented in the 2018 Netflix series *Wild Wild Country*. Unfortunately, the Netflix documentary was heavy on the craziness of the commune and very, very light on how the property ended up in the hands of Young Life. I was brought in early on in this transition to spearhead the spiritual cleansing of this property. Why such cleansing was needed was obvious to anyone who had visited the place. It was one of the creepiest places I've ever been, complete with secret underground tunnels and laboratories, a crematorium, and a huge indoor meeting area where the Bhagwan taught his thousands of followers. When workers tore down the podium from where he taught, they found a den of rattlesnakes underneath.

And just in case anyone doubted that the place was a demonic stronghold, while Young Life was in the process of acquiring the property, a wildfire broke out on a ridge to the north. While the fire threatened all the existing structures and infrastructure, it inexplicably stayed up on the ridge. Except for one tongue of flame that descended the ridge and burned to the ground a single structure: Bhagwan's personal residence, where he watched videos and took hits from his personal supply of nitrous oxide before driving through daily gatherings of his followers in one of his 93 Rolls Royces.

After the fire, all that remained was the chrome spigot that dispensed the laughing gas.

Over 20 years and thousands of campers later, most visitors don't know about the Bhagwan legacy. But to those involved in the handing-it-over phase of the ranch, it remains a vivid reminder of the reality of a spiritual battle that endures.

Finding A Balance

Spiritual warfare can be a controversial topic. Few Christians will argue over whether or not we're engaged in a battle with Satan and his demons while we go about our mission of advancing the Kingdom of God. They know we are. But the controversy emerges in the details: how demons work against us, how frequently we actually encounter them in daily living, and how we are to most effectively engage in the battle through prayer.

A pendulum never stops in the middle; it just passes through the center on its way from one side to the other. So also, the church has tended to swing from one side to the other in our understanding of spiritual warfare. Satan and his hordes are either little red devils with pitchforks who dance around mostly unnoticed, on the edges of our lives, or they are the controlling force behind virtually everything that goes wrong in the world.

So, let's start with where we can all agree: Scripture. We all realize the battle for the souls of young people is not merely "against flesh and blood, but against the rulers, against the authorities, against the powers of this dark world and against the spiritual forces of evil in the heavenly realms" (Eph. 6:12). And as we engage in this battle, we're aware of demonic schemes "in order that Satan might not outwit us" (2 Cor. 2:11).

On a corporate level, Satan strategy is to trash the Church, rendering it ineffective by any means possible. The evidence reveals his strategy works, at least for now: denominational battles; local church struggles, factions and splits; competition rather than cooperation and collaboration among organizations or within communities. On a personal level, Satan's strategy includes trashing us and our relationship with God, keeping us in spiritual darkness and bondage, and rendering us ineffective for Kingdom work. He'll do that by:

- Temptation (Mt. 4:1-11; 1 Cori. 7:5; 1 Thess. 3:5).
- False accusation (Rev. 12:10).
- Physical affliction (2 Cor. 12:7-10; the book of Job).
- Deceiving by subtly twisting God's truth (2 Cor. 11:13-15; 1 Jn. 4:1-3; 2 Jn. 7-11).
- Dividing relationships (Eph. 4:25-27; 2 Cor.2:10-11).
- Opposing us in ministry (Acts 13:6-12).
- Getting us to ignore or downplay the degree and subtlety of his influence (2 Cor. 2:11), which makes the aforementioned strategies all the more effective!

An additional strategy of the enemy introduces FUD into our hearts. In *Christian Prayer for Dummies* (Wiley, 2003), author Richard Wagner elaborates:

In the marketing world, FUD is a term that refers to the practice of using disinformation as a weapon against your competitors. For example, a salesperson who is trying to make a sale against a rival company might employ FUD by stressing the inherent soundness and safety of her company's product versus the Fear, Uncertainty, and Doubt (FUD) that would ensue if one chose the competitor's product. In the same way, Satan runs his own disinformation campaign in a Christian's life by using fear, uncertainty, and doubt as a competitive weapon against God. He'd prefer that you trust the world's security instead of relying on God, and he'll use FUD to win.

We're engaged in ministry to youth because we understand the strategic nature of what we do: the vast majority of decisions for Christ occur before the age of 20. Guess who else knows that? In my early years of youth ministry, the success of our ministry at reaching unchurched youth in our community was accompanied by stuff that I would clearly recognize as spiritual attack now. But at the time, I had little clue, until a friend steered me towards one of the few books about spiritual warfare in print at that time.

As I sat in my office and began to read, I experienced what I would describe as a "power encounter" with the enemy. A sudden, overwhelming fear gripped me as the hair on my arms stood on end, and I found it increasingly difficult to breathe. Discernment wasn't one of my stronger gifts, but I knew I wasn't alone in that room. So, did I slap on the full armor and stand against the devil's schemes (Eph. 6:11)? Nope. I freaked. Bolting from my chair, I ran out the door and down the sidewalk, gasping for breath.

I did eventually get my act together, and in personal encounters with the enemy in the ensuing years, I've been able to engage with a measure of effectiveness. But if there is one transforming truth I've learned about spiritual warfare that I have learned in recent years—and as is often the case, I learned it from my wife—that has made a world of difference, it is a biblical understanding of the spiritual protection and covering I have in Christ, because of His finished work on the Cross.

Christ the Victor

I've learned the hard way that one of the pitfalls of being an author is that, down the road, I may no longer believe something I published earlier. In an earlier book I wrote about a particularly stressful ministry assignment. Referring to spiritual warfare, a friend commented to me, "I hope you can deal with that huge bull's eye you now have on your back, Higgs." Back then I wrote that the comment turned out to be "both accurate and insightful." Twenty years later, maybe not so much. The comment isn't neces- sarily untrue regarding the bull's eye—how that actually works, I haven't a clue—but regardless, we don't have to deal with it. Christ did that for us! It's critical that we understand this, and teach it to our ministry spheres: youth workers, volunteers, young people, and their parents.

Spiritual protection is a significant theme runs throughout the Bible. This verse, while not traditionally thought of as a spiritual warfare passage, brings clarity: "When you were dead in your sins and in the uncircumcision of your sinful nature, God made you alive with Christ. He forgave us all our sins, having canceled the written code, with its regulations, that was against us and that stood opposed to us; he took it away, nailing it to the cross. And having disarmed the powers and authorities, he made a public spec- tacle of them, triumphing over them by the cross" (Col. 2:13-15).

Jesus' death on the Cross, and subsequent resurrection, defeated Satan and his power-and-authority minions. He didn't defeat them "kind of," until He shows up at the end of the Tribulation to bind Satan in the Abyss and then again, at the Final Battle when Satan is released to deceive the nations one final (and short!) time before he's banished to his eternal destination. His victory took place on the Cross, it was consummated at the Resurrection, and for those who by faith follow Christ today, Satan is a defeated foe. This was true for the Old Testament saints: "Now faith is being sure of what we hope for and certain of what we do not see. This is what the ancients were commended for" (Heb. 11:1-2), and it's true for us today:

> The Lord is a refuge for the oppressed, a stronghold in times of trouble. Those who know your name will trust in You, for You, Lord, have never forsaken those who seek You. (Ps. 9:9-10)

You are my hiding place; you will protect me from trouble and surround me with songs of deliverance. (Ps. 32:7)

God is our refuge and strength, an ever-present help in trouble. Therefore, we will not fear, though the earth gives way and the mountains fall into the heart of the sea, though its waters roar and foam and the mountains quake with their surging. (Ps. 46:1-3)

"I saw Satan fall like lightning from heaven. I have given you authority to trample on snakes and scorpions and to overcome all the power of the enemy; nothing will harm you." (Lk. 10:19)

In addition to all this, take up the shield of faith with which you can extinguish all the flaming arrows of the evil one. (Eph. 6:16)

But the Lord is faithful, and he will strengthen and protect you from the evil one. (2 Thess. 3:3)

The Lord will rescue me from every evil attack and will bring me safely to His heavenly Kingdom. (2 Tim. 4:18)

It is important—indeed, critical—to understand that this level of protection is available to every believer, but it requires faith and obedience. Psalm 18 is very instructive in this regard, enough that it warrants a closer look. Here, David asserted his confidence in God's protection: "I love you, O LORD, my strength. The LORD is my rock, my fortress and my deliverer; my God is my rock, in whom I take refuge. He is my shield and the horn of my salvation, my stronghold. I call to the LORD, who is worthy of praise, and I am saved from my enemies" (vs. 1-3).

David continues by describing an attack he experienced (vs. 4-5), his response of calling on the Lord for help (v. 6), God's awesome and powerful arrival on the scene (vs. 7-15), and his rescue: "He reached down from on high and took hold of me; he drew me out of deep waters. He rescued me from my powerful enemy, from my foes, who were too strong for me (vs. 16-17).

Yet, spiritual protection isn't a "given" to all Christians. There are responsibilities we fulfill to gain access to God's stronghold. David makes this clear:

> The LORD has dealt with me according to my righteousness; according to the cleanness of my hands he has rewarded me. For I have kept the ways of the LORD; I have not done evil by turning from my God. All his laws are before me; I have not turned away from his decrees. I have been blameless before him and have kept myself from sin. The LORD has rewarded me according to my righteousness, according to the cleanness of my hands in his sight. (vs. 20-24)

What kept David protected? What keeps you and me, and the kids we work with, safe within the stronghold of God? Holy living, confessing sin quickly and completely so we don't give the enemy a foothold (Eph. 4:26-27), and living obediently. When we live in that place, we not only receive defensive protection, we gain new offensive authority. We can "scale walls" (v. 29), "bend a bow of bronze" (v. 34), and our enemies will "turn their backs in flight" (v. 40).

The Apostle John sums this up succinctly and clearly: "We know that anyone born of God does not continue to sin; the one who was born of God keeps him safe and the evil one cannot harm him" (1 Jn. 5:18).

Leaving Room for Mystery

Truth be told, some mystery hides in spiritual warfare. Job is in the Bible for a reason; despite being "blameless and upright; he feared God and shunned evil" (Job 1:1), God gave Satan pretty devasting access to him. Paul, to keep him from conceit after a trip to the third heaven, received "a thorn in the flesh, a messenger of Satan to torment me" (2 Cor. 12:7). Jesus told Simon Peter that Satan asked to "sift you as wheat," (Lk. 22:31). This Greek word for "you" is plural—Satan sifted all the apostles.

Then there is the crazy prophecy from the prophet Micaiah to Ahab in 1 Kings:

> "Therefore, hear the word of the LORD: I saw the LORD sitting on his throne with all the host of heaven standing around him on his right and on his left. And the LORD said, 'Who will entice Ahab into attacking Ramoth Gilead and going to his death there?' One suggested this, and another that. Finally, a spirit came forward, stood before the LORD and said, 'I will entice him.' 'By what means?' the LORD asked. 'I will go out and be a lying spirit in the mouths of all his prophets,' he said. 'You will succeed in enticing him,' said the LORD. 'Go and do it.' So now the LORD has put a lying spirit in the mouths of all these prophets of yours. The LORD has decreed disaster for you."
> (1 Kgs. 22:19-23)

While many offer plausible, coherent, even reasonable explanations for these mysteries, Terri and I like to remember what an intercessor told us: "Satan is ever God's pawn." Yes, we are in an ongoing spiritual battle, and yes, we are to use the full armor of God in that battle (Eph. 6:10-17), which includes prayer! (More on that next chapter.) *Christus Victor* may be a Latin phrase for one of "theories of atonement" (which we will not get into here). The translation is both simple and accurate: Christ the Victor. He defeated Satan at the Cross. We are to walk in that victory, fearlessly. And teach students to do likewise.

Chapter 7

Praying for One Another

In the ongoing work of the kingdom of God, nothing is more important than Intercessory Prayer. People today desperately need the help that we can give them. Marriages are being shattered. Children are being destroyed. Individuals are living lives of quiet desperation, without purpose of future. And we can make a difference . . . if we will learn to pray on their behalf.

—RICHARD FOSTER

PAUL UNDERSTOOD the nature of the spiritual battle and our covering in Christ better than most, yet his writings are peppered with requests for prayer for protection:

> I urge you, brothers, by our Lord Jesus Christ and by the love of the Spirit, to join me in my struggle by praying to God for me. Pray that I may be rescued from the unbelievers in Judea and that my service in Jerusalem may be acceptable to the saints there. (Rom. 15:30-31)

> For I know that through your prayers and the help given by the Spirit of Jesus Christ, what has happened to me will turn out for my deliverance. (Phil. 1:19)

> And pray that we may be delivered from wicked and evil men, for not everyone has faith. (2 Thess. 3:2)

We do not want you to be uninformed, brothers, about
the hardships we suffered in the province of Asia. We
were under great pressure, far beyond our ability to endure,
so that we despaired even of life. Indeed, in our hearts
we felt the sentence of death. But this happened that we
might not rely on ourselves but on God, who raises the
dead. He has delivered us from such a deadly peril, and
he will deliver us. On him we have set our hope that he
will continue to deliver us, as you help us by your prayers.
Then many will give thanks on our behalf for the gracious
favor granted us in answer to the prayers of many.
(2 Cor. 1:8-11)

Although Paul knew his protection ultimately had its source in
Christ, he was also convinced that God would use the prayers of
His people to support that safeguard. This is clear in the familiar
Ephesians 6 passage concerning our spiritual armor. Paul takes
great pains to describe the elements of our armor: the belt of truth,
the breastplate of righteousness, the feet fitted with readiness
from the gospel, the shield of faith, the helmet of salvation, the
sword of the Spirit (vs. 14-17). We're afforded all this as we abide
in the stronghold of Christ. In fact, the armor is Christ Himself
(Rom.13:14). Yet, Paul follows this list with a description of prayer
for spiritual protection. It's a poignant passage because he's both
instructive and personal:

And pray in the Spirit on all occasions with all kinds of
prayers and requests. With this in mind, be alert and
always keep on praying for all the saints. Pray also for me,
that whenever I open my mouth, words may be given me
so that I will fearlessly make known the mystery of the
gospel, for which I am an ambassador in chains. Pray that I
may declare it fearlessly, as I should. (6:18-20)

While Scripture isn't clear concerning the extent to which Paul had an organized team of prayer supporters, it is obvious that the covering provided by the intercession of others should be mandatory for those in leadership. C. Peter Wagner writes, "The most underutilized source of spiritual power in our churches today is intercession for Christian leaders" (*Prayer Shield*, Regal Books, 1992, pg. 19).

Covering Your Family and Home

Our children are now grown and married, but when they lived at home and I traveled on ministry assignments, my family sometimes experienced a measure of spiritual harassment. And there were seasons when it was more than a measure. My wife would awaken in the night with a sense she was not alone; my son struggled with nightmares; my daughter tried to cope with a variety of fears. The attacks weren't always confined to my absence. I spent many nighttime hours praying through our home, interceding for my family, and engaging in direct warfare praying.

To be clear: since our family came to understand the biblical truth I wrote about in the last chapter regarding our spiritual protection in Christ, this kind of harassment diminished significantly. But the enemy will try to infiltrate our homes and families. Since he is a master of deceit and deception, attacks will often be subtle or in the form of something that could be explained away, i.e., sicknesses, nightmares, arguments, temptations. As I have struggled with discernment through these types of attacks, I have learned two additional principles (besides those covered in the last chapter) that have been quite helpful in this area.

First, I have been continually reminded that as the head of my household and family (See Eph. 5:23ff; 1 Tim. 2:11-14 concerning husbands; Eph. 6:1-3 and Col. 3:20 about children), I have the responsibility to provide, through my prayers, holy living and spiritual leadership, protection and covering for my family.

Second, I've learned if I ask, the Lord will show me (or my wife, or our intercessors, or even on occasion our children) if a particular problem at home is rooted in the wiles of the enemy or is simply a case of bad take-out food. Far too often, we dismiss or neglect symptoms indicative of spiritual harassment: chronic illness, including persistent nausea or headaches; disturbed or harassed children, heaviness lingering in the home; insomnia or unusual sleepiness; prolonged lack of peace; recurrent bad dreams and nightmares.

Part of our neglect stems from a legitimate desire not to give the enemy too much credit. However, the danger of giving the devil too much credit is, in my mind, dwarfed by the danger of not recognizing his schemes. A spiritually protected home and family is a wonderful place of refuge and rest, but we must realize that the enemy knows this, too, and will do all he can to disrupt it. But remember this (from the last chapter): he has no rights of disruption unless we abdicate our rights.

A Ministry Prayer Team

I hadn't been a Christian very long when I entered vocational youth ministry, so I hadn't the time to forget the basic tenets of the faith that I was taught, and experienced, as a new believer. One of those tenets concerned prayer: "No prayer, no power; some prayer, some power; much prayer, much power!" I thought that was reasonable theology back then, and I still do. Perhaps my motives were a bit more mixed than they are now: "No prayer, no success; some prayer, some success; much prayer, much success and fame!" Regardless, as a newly minted youth worker, I wanted to make sure our youth ministry included much prayer. So, I scheduled a regular prayer time for our volunteer team, Monday through Friday from 6:30 to 7:15 a.m., in the basement of a building that our church was working on converting into a community youth center.

I was naïve and idealistic, but for a year and a half I only missed two meetings, and I almost always had "two or more" (Mt. 18:20) with me, and often many more. We wrote Scripture on the bare sheetrock around us, and I kept a journal for recording our prayers and their answers. I still have the journal; one doesn't easily dispose of such an amazing record of God's faithfulness.

During that season of youthful exuberance, the prayer-power principle became embedded in my ministry DNA. But it wasn't until years later I realized "much prayer" meant not only me and my team, it also included "much prayer" from others committed to supporting us on a consistent. So, I went about developing a ministry prayer team.

Prayer Team Particulars

There are, I have discovered through trial and much error, a variety of ways to go about this. So rather that identify a particular model to follow, I would like to identify some guidelines I have gleaned over the years—mostly from others; notably C. Peter Wagner in his book *Prayer Shield*, (Regal Books, 2010) but also from my own experiences with prayer teams. I hope the guidelines will be helpful in creating your own working prayer team model.

Intentionally recruit prayer team members. At least two strategies work in this regard: 1) issuing a broad call for prayer support to your congregation, friends, and supporters, and 2) hand-picking and asking potential pray-ers personally. I've used a mix of both strategies. Because my wife and I currently lead a nonprofit organization, we started our recruiting by describing our needs in a monthly newsletter, and asking people to respond if they had an interest. To those who responded, we gave more details about what they were getting themselves into. If they felt the Lord leading them, they would join the team. Then, as time passed and we sensed the need for a deeper level of personal prayer support, we recruited a select group of people who resonated with our ministry assignments and challenges, and/or were wired/gifted as intercessors.

When I served as a local church youth pastor, I issued a broad call to our congregation for prayer support for our ministry. I sent special invitations to senior citizens, many of whom love to pray for kids, and to parents. When I identified the intercessors in the church, I aggressively pursued them. All of it was, and is, intentional. I know many youth workers who consistently ask their congregation to pray for them and their ministry. That's good! But it's not a substitute for the intentional development of a prayer team.

Quality is more important than quantity. A case can be made for the more, the merrier when it comes to prayer supporters. The late prayer movement leader and author Peter Wagner counted hundreds on his team, and the founder of Campus Crusade for Christ (now Cru), the late Bill Bright, estimated his team numbered in the thousands. Considering the size of their ministries, these numbers made sense. Our prayer team currently numbers around 40. We've found when our team approaches three figures, we lose the personal connection that, for us, forms an important component of our prayer support. As a local youth pastor, my prayer supporters usually numbered around a dozen, and that size worked great. Which do you think is more effective, a hundred people who pray for you on an occasional basis, or a dozen who pray on a consistent basis, even daily, and take the initiative to stay current concerning your personal and ministry prayer needs?

There can be different levels of a prayer team, depending on your degree of involvement in ministry, and your inquiring of the Lord. Wagner's support consisted of three levels of prayer supporters (see his book *Prayer Shield* for details), while we maintain two levels on our team. The point isn't the number of levels, but rather, the reason for different levels. Our Level One are folks committed to pray on a relatively consistent basis. They may not know all the details, but they pray, and we need them desperately. Level Two comprises a much smaller number of people who feel called to intercede for us more intentionally. These pray-ers need more information, so we communicate with them more regularly and in greater detail. When they hear from the Lord about our family or ministry, they let us know.

Communication is the key to your prayer team. In addition to our monthly ministry newsletter, our prayer team gets a regular Intercessors' Update that presents more prayer needs and answers to prayer. We try to keep it simple. (To be honest, when I receive a prayer letter with a lengthy list of requests, I usually don't cover them all.) We remind them to tell us what the Lord says to them about our family and ministry. In some circles, this is called a prophetic word, or "word" for short. Regardless of what it is called, I think most of us would agree God speaks to us through other people. On numerous occasions, intercessors from different parts of the country, who did not know each other, have given us identical prophetic words that were remarkably accurate. We do not take "words" from our prayer team lightly; time and again, God has spoken in significant and strategic ways through them.

Involvement on a prayer team is not a life-long commitment. It's good to give folks an "out" if they no longer can meet the commitments as prayer team members. Don't assume they'll let you know if they want off. They usually won't; they'll just quit praying. Occasionally, tell them to let you know if they can't continue. Express your gratitude for their prayer support, and release them with your blessing.

A prayer team is not the same as a financial support team.
Those of us who have the privilege of raising personal financial
support should make a clear distinction between our prayer supporters and our financial supporters. Often folks do both for us,
but it's unwise to assume financial are also prayer supporters,
or visa versa.

Having a committed, involved prayer team is both a tremendous encouragement and, at times, an invaluable asset. We're truly
better together!

SELAH

Upper Room Practitioners

As we transition from Personal Prayer to Corporate Prayer, it's the appropriate time for another Selah—this time to hear from some Practitioners. This Selah was motivated in part by a few honest questions I had to ask myself when preparing to write this book: Do I have any remaining "street cred" when it comes to youth ministry? Do my experience and perspective compensate for the lack of recent hands-on work "in the trenches" with teenagers or involvement in a youth group? Since I don't really know the answers, I've solicited the help of friends who work in the trenches doing real youth ministry. And doing it well.

After moving to Idaho, I often commuted back to Portland almost monthly for close to 10 years, primarily to invest in about 18 gender and ethnically diverse young youth ministry leaders. Jarin Oda and Keithen Schwahn belonged to this cohort, called The Portland Collective, as well as another smaller, more intimate gathering called The Young Lions. They're lions of the faith, with humility and wisdom beyond their years. I've not known Phil Togwell and Olivia Williamson as well or as long, but they're highly recommended, with similar character traits. All four are radical practitioners of the faith, and true prayer warriors.

Jarin Oda:
The Practice of Prayer

Jarin serves as the Pastor of Youth at the Bridgetown Church in Portland, Oregon, where he resides with his wife, Grace. He was born and raised on the island of Oahu, Hawaii, and aims to live and lead in the way of Jesus.

PRAYER, IN ALL sincerity, is my safest *and* most frustrating rhythm of my daily connection with Jesus. Prayer is my safest rhythm of connection with Jesus because it was my first memorable act of faith when I encountered His felt presence in prayer at age 15. The memory of realizing the Jewish Rabbi of the First Century was still alive, knew my name, and affectionately loved me, has marked my life of prayer for the past 13 years.

That said, there have been legitimate ebbs and flows in my consistency with prayer, as well as the noticeable ebb and flows of the Lord's felt presence during time with Him. Still, years later, prayer has been my first act of visible faith in Jesus, alongside my morning cup of coffee and the Scriptures. "We cannot make Him visible to us, but we can make ourselves visible to Him," said Rabbi Abraham Joshua Heschel (*Prayer*, 1945). Prayer is my primary way to make myself visible to Jesus.

Practically, on most days, I pray the Lord's Prayer (Mt. 6:9-13) in the morning, intercede for the lost at midday, and say a gratitude prayer in the evening, following my Church's Daily Prayer Rhythms. Furthermore, I aim to pray the Jesus Prayer out loud at least five times throughout the day. That ancient prayer says, "O Lord Jesus Christ, Son of God, have mercy on me, a sinner." This helps me to re-center my attention and adoration to Jesus in the midst of the many obligations and distractions each day brings.

Rhythm and Frustration

Prayer is also my most frustrating rhythm of connection with Jesus because it regularly uncovers the gamut of my doubts about God's existence, my fear of being disappointed or let down by Him, and my ache in being frequently distracted in the "boring" quiet of prayer. While the daily act of prayer acknowledges my need for God by the very act of asking for His presence, it also uncovers the places in life where I aspire to self-reliance and control. Irony is the only word I can use to express the tension of my daily prayer life!

There are, however, a plethora of wiser and older spiritual leaders who validate the tension I find in my prayer by their own stories. One of these spiritual leaders, author Philip Yancey, describes the tension of prayer: "Most of my struggles in the Christian life circle around the same two themes: why God doesn't act the way we want God to, and why I don't act the way God wants me to. Prayer is the precise point where those themes converge" (*Prayer: Does It Make Any Difference?* Zondervan 2016). Tyler Staton, pastor of the Bridgetown Church, explains, "Prayer doesn't resolve our anxiety. Prayer itself makes us anxious because it uncovers fears we can ignore as long as we don't engage deeply, thoughtfully, vulnerably with God" (*Praying Like Monks, Living Like Fools,* Zondervan 2022).

Prayer is, in my life, my safest and most frustrating rhythm of daily connection with Jesus. And I'm coming to learn that irony doesn't discount prayer. It legitimizes it.

Keithen Schwahn:
Presence over Program

Keithen devotes his life to reversing the narrative that young people are a lost cause in the Church. From an indigenous family in Wyoming, he now lives in New York City as a pastor at the Church of the City New York. He's building a network of leaders and launching YTH.NYC. Keithen and his wife, Celeste, contend for the next great move of God in our time, and enjoy coffee and walks in the West Village.

A YEAR AND a half into high-school youth ministry in Portland, I hit a wall. This wall wasn't burnout, exhaustion, or a loss of passion or drive. The wall I hit was heartbreak. I had invested my everything into what I thought was the model for successful youth ministry, and it was booming! Hundreds of students, a massive leadership team, a large budget, huge events, amazing worship bands, and catchy topical teaching. Our youth night was the place to be. West Portland high schools knew about us, students loved us, and, in our minds, we were rolling. And yet after everything we had invested, the environment we had created, and the number of students who were attending, our hearts broke as we watched more of our seniors walk away from their faith than remained faithful to Jesus as they graduated and went to university.

Something Had to Change

My longtime youth ministry teammate decided to step out of ministry, which sent our team into a rebuild. Our new staff and I started to ask the simple question, "Why are we doing what we are doing?" Our team concluded that most of our youth night struc-ture, event programing, and overall ministry priorities were shaped not by the living presence of God, but rather by previous models of ministry we inherited. They had become the very definition of old wineskins (Mt. 9:16-17). The Holy Spirit invited us into a rebuild, centered not around the programs we could pull off in the flesh, but around His presence. What would a movement of young people in a city look like if we removed much of what resembled modern youth ministry? Turns out, it looked a lot like prayer.

Dallas Willard once defined prayer as "conversing with God about what we are experiencing and doing together." Under this framework, prayer is *relationship*, *adventure*, and *partnership* with God. We found that connecting students to God Himself was far better than trying to create a loosely Christian-flavored consumeristic environment for young people. And we found when we created space for encounter, and expected to see the movement of God among us, our young people came alive.

From Attraction to Relationship

First, we moved the purpose of our gatherings from attraction to relationship. The first question we used to ask was, "How do we run attractional events to minster to students and introduce them to Jesus?" This isn't a bad question, but I found that the answer throws the central focus of the ministry off from the beginning. In the Hebrew Scriptures, the role of the priests was to "minister to God" (Deut. 10:8). Yet most of our responsibilities as youth pastors is to "minister to students." This places the primary focus of our ministry on the young people we lead, rather than on God's voice and presence. What if our primarily focus was on Him, and then on creating a family of young people similarly obsessed with hosting the living presence of God? That their only aim was to seek Him, hear Him, and respond to Him in ways that would please Him? As Jesus said about the Father in John 8:29: ". . . for I always do what pleases Him."

Practically, this looks like starting every youth night with 30 minutes of worship and prayer, and ending with a half hour or more in worship and prayer to cap the night. For some, this may seem like a wasteful amount of time to pray and worship, yet we found focusing on meeting with God, instead of simply talking about Him and about our issues, created an environment where students were being transformed. So the focus of our youth nights became hosting His presence, and we planned and prioritized accordingly.

From Routine to Adventure

Second, leaning in to host God's presence, we found that our gatherings never looked the same again. Each time we met, if we listened closely, God had unique things say that would lead us on an adventure instead of getting stuck in routine. As we created a praying environment in the 30 minutes before the official start time of youth night, we began asking God if He had anything specific that He wanted us to do that night. We would sit in silence for a season, listening for His voice and any specific invitations from the Spirit. We would then take a few minutes and interact regarding how we sensed God may be leading us that night.

These feedback times started broad with a student or leader sharing something like, "God just wants everyone here to know they're loved." Which is true, and is a great first step, but as we continued to create the space to listen and step out in faith, we found that the words of prophecy and words of knowledge and calls for unique healing got more and more specific. This created an adventure dynamic with our students. They started showing up asking, "What is God going to do tonight?" rather than looking to old routines of youth ministry and asking, "What are the leaders planning for us tonight, and will it be any good?" Leaning into the Spirit created excitement and expectation for a fresh encounter each youth night.

Striving to Partnering

Last, we saw a pattern emerging around burnout and turnover among youth pastors and leaders. The pace and emotional weight of leading the typical youth ministry often isn't sustainable for long term. Accordingly, the average lifespan of a youth pastor in a particular ministry is only around two to three years. Our team started to ask, "Why?" What about this particular role in the church causes so many to become disillusioned and exhausted?

The answer? We needed to move from a place of striving to run a ministry, to partnering with God about how He wanted to lead our group. The prophet Zechariah spoke prophetically over a new king rising to reign over the returning nation of Judah after the Babylonian exile. The prophet declared this leadership would lead "not by might, nor by power, but by my spirit says the Lord" (Zech. 4:6). In our rebuilding moment, we needed to completely strip back our approach and ask, "What is built in striving ("might and power"), and what is built by God ("by my Spirit.")?

We discovered that presence-centered ministry is far more sustainable, and fights against burnout, as the pressure to lead falls not on an individual or pastoral staff, but on the Spirit of God. We simply partner with God in what He wants to do in the lives of our students. Practically, this looked like running a much simpler calendar than before, with an ongoing emphasis on hearing God and responding to His movement. And instead of jumping in to try to fix every situation, we created space for prayer ministry. We told our students, "We don't have what it takes to heal or fix the trauma or pain of your life, but we know the One who does."

Prayer wasn't a five-minute afterthought at the end of the night, or quickly going around the circle for prayer requests. Nor was it saying, "I'll pray for you this week," then not really doing so. Partnering with God meant we spent long periods of time in prayer over difficult situations, rather than jumping in to fix things. We found this approach so much lighter and more freeing for our team and our leaders.

I learned so much from hitting that wall, and the experience of having my heart broken. By the time I handed off my ministry, after four years of centering on the Presence, many seniors were graduating as people marked the Presence. They weren't pointing back to fun experiences they had, created by a team of caring leaders within a budget. Rather, they were pointing back to hearing God, seeing Him move, and loving an environment where they felt empowered to participate. Now, eight years later, I'm building a similar environment in New York City and watching prayer capture the imaginations of Generation Z unlike anything else. It turns out the simple ancient path actually leads to life (Jer. 6:16) and young people are continuing to encounter God through prayer.

Will more of us create space for His *presence* over our *programs*?

Olivia Williamson:
Claim Your Campus

Olivia Williamson is the director of Claim Your Campus, a school prayer ministry, and the founder of Enlightened Students, a high-school worship movement. She's also an engaging preacher and singer-songwriter musician. She currently resides in Kansas City with her husband, Kyle. With a heart for prayer and this next generation, she loves to help people identify two things: God's voice and their calling in life.

IT WAS THE first time I had seen her. She had the brightest pink hair I've ever seen. It shocked me that I had never noticed her before at my school. Thankfully, she found our small prayer group that morning.

Every week, a group of 10 to 12 students would meet outside our high school cafeteria to pray. We symbolically left a hole in our circle for someone. This day she filled that hole.

She shared how she didn't want to be at home or school. There wasn't a place where she felt a sense of belonging. When she sat with us, we shared Jesus' love with her. We prayed over her just a few moments before school started. Heaven touched that circle as tears streamed down her face.

I got to experience powerful moments of ministry in my school because of this prayer group called Claim Your Campus. Because of what I witnessed then, I have a deeper understanding and passion for calling the next generation to do the same!

Back in 2003, a world-changing prayerwalk took place in America. Little did they know, a small praying group of high school students in Michigan would birth a national student-led prayer movement. After an initial prayerwalk, the group experienced a growing desire to pray for their school regularly. They asked their youth pastor when they could gather again. He encouraged them to meet weekly in their school themselves. So they did.

After some time, the group realized they didn't know what exactly to pray about when they gathered. The youth pastor challenged his students to think of one issue that negatively impacted the student body. Together, they discussed and discovered an issue their campus faced that needed change. Fights broke out every day in the halls. They began to pray persistently for an end to fighting in their school.

After weeks of intercession, the youth pastor heard astounding news from his lead pastor, who attended a school board meeting. School officials reported that for some unknown reason, the fighting stopped. The lead pastor knew why. The youth pastor knew why. A group of eight young intercessors knew why the fighting stopped. The youth pastor asked the question, "What if this happened in every school in America?"

A Vision for Schools

After this small beginning, God downloaded a vision in this youth pastor's mind for students in every middle and high school in America to pray weekly for change. If 15 students in every school prayed, one million young intercessors would cover the land in prayer. Since then, that youth pastor, Geoff Eckart, said "yes" to doing anything he could to teach students to pray. Over the years, he's heard and read thousands of stories from across the nation about the results of young people praying.

In 2009, Eckart officially founded Claim Your Campus (CYC) under an umbrella organization called Never The Same, a national youth ministry reaching thousands of churches and students. Since 2009, more than 30,000 students have felt called to start prayer groups and have been trained through Claim Your Campus resources. They're trained at churches, CYC gatherings, national conferences, through a prayer app, and virtual training calls.

In 2021, I officially stepped in as director of Claim Your Campus. I felt intimidated to follow Eckart's footsteps and fulfill the task ahead. But I'd clearly seen God move powerfully through this generation in so many ways. No question, He can call one million students to prayer! Through partnerships with other ministries, unity in the Church, and connection with students, we're watching God bless our efforts.

When I stepped into this role, I strongly felt students should be taught to pray. Students don't need to feel intimidated about talking with God. When they learn more, they gain confidence and an urgency to intercede for their spheres of influence. God wields the power to change people and circumstances, but when students pray, He also transforms their hearts.

CYC is a student-led movement because students hold the right and authority to pray for their schools. They know the ins and outs of their campuses. Students who meet in groups pray specifically for issues they or their friends face daily. Prayer is an organic and simple way Christians can impact their peers and teachers.

Middle and high schoolers can join the movement in three easy steps:

Download the Claim Your Campus app.
Invite two or more friends to pray, or pray with an already existing Christian club.
Show up and pray weekly.

Adults Can Get Involved

The movement needs mentors, parents, pastors, and teachers to share Claim Your Campus with more students. Share the three steps to join CYC and pray for the impact on students. Consider prayerwalking a school with families, parents, pastors and students with the CYC Prayerwalk Guide. Support schools on the outside while students study and pray on the inside. Go to www.

claimyourcampus.com/prayerwalk to learn more about prayerwalks and a free Prayerwalk Guide.

Imagine a praying generation ushering in revival to every corner of the United States. The stories of healing, revival, and transformation would be endless. Schools would be shining cities on a hill because students live in the power and presence of Jesus Christ.

Lord, we ask for student-led prayer in every middle and high school, in our day!

Phil Togwell:
Prayer Spaces in Schools

Phil and Emma Togwell live on the North East coast of England with their extended family of daughters, foster-mums-and-babies, lodgers, and dogs. Phil trained and worked in a variety of youth and community settings before being hijacked by the 24-7 Prayer Movement, where he now serves the global team by leading Prayer Spaces in Schools and writing for the Lectio app.

ACCORDING TO THE Gospel writers, Jesus' disciples only asked Him to teach them one thing: how to pray. If I'd been there, I probably would've asked Jesus for tips on raising the dead or feeding crowds of people. I'd want to know how to feed thousands with just a few sandwiches, a packet of ready-salted chips, and a brownie. (If I hadn't already eaten them). But they asked Him to teach them to pray.

The disciples almost certainly prayed every day. They would've learned a lot about prayer from their families and religious leaders. And yet, when they witnessed Jesus praying, they saw something profoundly different. I wonder what they saw? Simplicity? Honesty? Intimacy? Power and authority? Whatever the disciples observed, they knew they didn't have it, and they wanted to have it more than anything else.

"When you come before God, don't turn that into a theatrical production, . . ." said Jesus in response to their request, perhaps having a bit of a dig at the professional religious leaders nearby. "Do you think God sits in a box seat?" He added with a smile. "Find a place where you won't be tempted to role-play before God." Getting down to business, He added, "Just be there as simply and honestly as you can manage. The focus will shift from you to God, and you will begin to sense his grace."

"This is your Father you are dealing with," Jesus explained, bringing His brief instructions to a conclusion, "And He knows better than you what you need. With a God like this loving you, you can pray very simply. Like this . . . " (Mt. 6; 5-6, MSG).

Somehow, somewhere along the way, we've made this prayer thing a lot more complicated than Jesus meant it to be, especially for children and young people. It may be because we, as adults, don't find it easy to "be there, simply and honestly" ourselves. We over complicate things instead of keeping them simple; we pray what we think we ought to pray instead of being honest about what's really going on in our lives. And then we teach our children and young people lots *about* prayer, rather than encouraging them to just try praying.

If we want young people to know the "God like this loving (them)," and to "sense his grace" (vs. 8) in life-transforming ways, I think we need to make some changes. We need to try some new ways to help them connect with God, simply and honestly. One of the ways that seems to work is to use creative prayer activities.

Prayer Spaces in Schools

For the last 15 years or so, Prayer Spaces in Schools, a ministry of the 24-7 Prayer movement, has been training and equipping Christians to turn classrooms into simple, hospitable prayer spaces for a few days at a time. Each prayer space typically has a selection of eight to ten creative prayer activities, with themes from the students' everyday lives. Themes like asking big questions, expressing gratitude, letting go of worry, resolving conflict, saying sorry, that kind of thing.

These prayer activities are all rooted in the words and ways of Jesus, and (like Jesus) they allow students to come as they are, whether they have faith or not, and engage in whatever way makes sense to them. So far, more than a million children and young people have participated in a prayer space in their schools, and we've witnessed thousands, perhaps tens of thousands, responding to the invitation to "try praying." The stories from these prayer spaces amaze us. For example:

> "Using the Post-it notes was really helpful. It gave me a way to pray. It was the first time I prayed properly."
>
> —15-year-old Student

> "I've never seen prayer displayed or experienced like this before. It's made me realize how many different ways prayer can be recited. It's opened up religion into my life again. Thank you!"
>
> —17-year-old Student

> "It was really fun. It made me see God everywhere I look. God spoke to me."
>
> —11-year-old Student

> "It felt like the truth in here."
>
> —11-year-old Student

After tracking and supporting more than 5,000 prayer spaces in all sorts of schools—church schools and public schools, elementary and high schools, within the UK and in more than 30 other nations—we've noticed that the prayer activities that work really well have a few things in common.

None of these things are new, of course, and most can be seen in what Jesus taught, and in the way He taught. So, whether you're a parent wanting to encourage your own children to grow in prayer, or a youth worker wanting to deepen the prayer lives of those in your group, or someone motivated a pioneer a prayer space in a school, these questions can assist when creating prayer activities.

Is it simple? Is your prayer activity, or whatever you're doing to invite young people to pray, simple? Can you explain it in one sentence, without using abstract concepts or religious words? If so, this is a great place to start. You're on the right track. Remember Jesus' words: "With a God like this loving you, you can pray very simply . . ." (vs. 8).

Is it real? Is it relevant? Start with what's going on in the lives of your young people. What are they angry or sad about, confused by, excited about, struggling with, worried about? Your prayer activity needs to begin with something—a theme or experience—that young people can relate to. Jesus talked with ordinary people about their everyday lives. For example, He talked about farming and fishing with farmers and fisherman. He helped them connect with God from the context of their immediate lives and concerns.

Is it interactive? Prayer means more than words. In fact, our words sometimes get in the way of simple, honest communication with God. I once heard prayer described as soul talk, a kind of communication that doesn't always require words. That makes a lot of sense to me. What helps young people express what's really going on inside them? Dancing? Drawing? Playing music? Running? Singing? Making things, or destroying them? How about blowing kisses?

My brother has cerebral palsy. He is able to control his electric wheelchair, but his body is so severely twisted and his muscles so wasted that he's unable to care for himself in any way. He's never been able to speak, never been able to put into words what he's thinking or feeling. But for as long as I can remember, whenever my dad has taken him along to the local Anglican church services, Matthew has blown kisses throughout the prayers and worship. Is he "saying" something when he blows kisses? Of course he is. But what is he saying? Nobody really knows. Does anybody need to know? No. Does God know what's going on? Yes!

My point: it's okay to use words when we pray, of course, but with young people, it's best to include a mix of wordy and non-wordy activities. The best prayer activities involve something to reflect on and something to do in response. For example, drop that, make this, move that, tear this, tie this, walk over there, wipe that, write this. If it's fun or exciting, that's even better.

Is it inclusive? Jesus was angry with His disciples when He saw they were pushing children to the back of the crowd. "Let them come to me . . ." (Mk.10:14) He demanded. Jesus welcomed everyone, and He still does. Jesus is hospitable and open-hearted toward all, regardless of their cultural background, academic ability, and even how they describe their faith, or lack of it. Is your prayer activity, or whatever you're doing to invite young people to pray, hospitable and welcoming? A prayer activity—and prayer itself—can sometimes be challenging, but it should never exclude.

Is it "take-away-able?" Is it "sticky?" I know that "take-away-able" isn't a real word, but you know what I mean. Will young people be able to repeat the prayer activities in their own time and space? Will they learn things as well as experience things? Will the prayer time stick with them? A simple way to encourage this is to create prayer activities using items young people find at home, or will see every day.

Is it personal and communal? Do your prayer activities provide opportunities for personal reflection and solitude, and also for dialogue and companionship with others? As Jesus demonstrated, sometimes we need to "go it alone" in prayer, and other times when we need friends to go with us.

Is it like Jesus? I couldn't think of a better way to phrase this question, but what I mean is this: Are you clear about how prayer activities reflect the words or ways of Jesus? Prayer activities don't need proof text verses to validate them, especially in schools. But it's important that we know why we're doing what we're doing. For example, 'Big Questions' is my favorite prayer activity to use in schools. It invites young people, whether they believe in God or not, to imagine He sits at the table in front of them. And then it asks, "What is the one question you would like to ask Him?" When I introduce this activity to a group I admit that I have questions, too. Sometimes, I explain that many of the people in the Bible prayed Big Question prayers, including Jesus Himself, so we are in good company. The Big Questions children and young people ask are often wonderfully unfiltered—honest, heart-breaking, angry, searching, even funny. I think God is OK with prayers like this.

Is it two-way? Perhaps, more than anything else, it was the intimacy of Jesus' relationship with His Father, and the way He listened for and heard His Father's voice, that the disciples wanted to learn for themselves. The way He listened for and heard His Father's voice. Prayer is two-way communication, so this is an important question to consider: do your prayer activities provide opportunities for children and young people to pause, be still, and listen *for* the Father's voice? And what will they do when God speaks?

Postscript: Prayer Activity Resources

The www.prayerspacesinschools.com website presents loads of free-to-download prayer activities, using simple, everyday objects, including fizzy tablets, Love Heart sweets, a life-size Tardis (from the Doctor Who series), an Olympic hurdle, zips (zippers), and even a wheelbarrow. If you Google "prayer activity ideas" you'll find hundreds of other ideas, too. There's no shortage of stuff. The thing is to get started with the children and young people you know. Teach them to pray.

PART THREE

The Upper Room of Acts: Corporate Prayer

CORPORATE PRAYER in synagogues and the temple was an integral part of the Jewish prayer rhythm during the time of Jesus. There are instructions about corporate prayer in the gospels (Mt. 18:19-20), and we can assume at least some group prayer was a part of Jesus discipleship regimen with His followers (Acts 1:14). But there are no clear examples of the contents of corporate prayer found in the four gospel accounts.

This changes radically in the book of Acts. After the resurrected Jesus instructs His followers to wait for the baptism of the Holy Spirit, and then ascends to heaven, they immediately head back to the Upper Room in Jerusalem where they were staying, and "they all joined together constantly in prayer" (Acts 1:14).

What were they praying about? Scripture is not clear about that, but since they must have been pretty confused about what to do next, plus wondering what in the world being "baptized by the Holy Spirit" meant, one can imagine their prayer was both desperate and hopeful.

Then when the Holy Spirit does come, with the power Jesus promised, everything changes. The New Testament Church is born, and corporate prayer becomes one of the four primary expressions—along with the apostles' teaching, fellowship, and the breaking of bread—of their early gatherings (Acts 2:42). After Peter and John were released following interrogation by the Sanhedrin, the early Church "raised their voices together in prayer to God . . . after they prayed, the place where they were meeting was shaken. And they were all filled with the Holy Spirit and spoke the word of God boldly" (Acts 4:24, 31). When Peter was later arrested and imprisoned by Herod, "The church was earnestly praying to God for him" (Acts 12:5), which led to his miraculous release. Paul and Barnabas were sent out on their first missionary journey by corporate prayer and fasting (Acts 13:2-3).

References to, and requests for, corporate prayer scatter throughout the Epistles. (Some examples: Rom. 12;12; 15:30-32; 2 Cor. 1:10-11; Eph. 6:18-20; Phil. 1:19, 4:6; Col. 4:2-4; 1 Thess. 5:17, 25; 2 Thess. 3:1-2; Heb. 13:18-19; Jude 20.)

There is something powerful about corporate prayer. Jesus' pattern on how to pray, The Lord's Prayer (Matt. 6:9-13; Luke 11:1-4), repeatedly uses the plural pronouns "our" and "us." While it certainly can be used for personal prayer, apparently the primary application relates to corporate prayer. And Jesus emphasized the spiritual power that emerges from agreement in prayer:

> "I tell you the truth, whatever you bind on earth will be bound in heaven, and whatever you loose on earth will be loosed in heaven. Again, I tell you that if two of you on earth agree about anything you ask for, it will be done for you by my Father in heaven. For where two or three come together in my name, there am I with them." (Mt. 18:18-20)

Corporate prayer can be tricky in youth ministry. New believers, or even long-time followers of Christ, can (and do!) get nervous about praying out loud in a group setting. Participants in groups prayer can get confused or frustrated about knowing what is appropriate to say out loud in prayer. Sustaining group prayer beyond a few minutes, or keeping it focused, can be a challenge. But let's look at it all as rehearsals for one of the last examples of corporate prayer, praise, and worship we find in Scripture:

> Then I heard what sounded like a great multitude, like the roar of rushing waters and like loud peals of thunder, shouting: "Hallelujah! For our Lord God Almighty reigns. Let us rejoice and be glad and give him glory! For the wedding of the Lamb has come, and his bride has made herself ready. Fine linen, bright and clean, was given her to wear". . . Amen. Come, Lord Jesus. (Rev. 19:6-8; 22:20)

Chapter 8

Creating a Culture of Prayer

The men upon whose shoulders rested the initial respon-
sibility of Christianizing the world came to Jesus with
one supreme request. They did not say, "Lord, teach us to
preach," "Lord, teach us to do miracles," or "Lord, teach us
to be wise" . . . but they said, "Lord, teach us to pray."

—BILLY GRAHAM

TWO ESSENTIALS turn a youth ministry into a praying youth ministry. We covered the first essential, both implicitly and explicitly, in
earlier chapters: a praying youth leader. The second essential is creating a culture of prayer. But before we accelerate into the specifics
of that, let's tap the brakes for just a minute. Just as a praying youth
leader is the end product when a leader is passionately in love with
Jesus and living a holy, obedient life, a culture of prayer is the end
product when those involved in the youth ministry are similarly
passionate about loving Jesus and living in a way that pleases Him.
Richard J. Foster, in the opening pages of his modern-day classic,
Prayer: Finding the Heart's True Home, elaborates on this love:

> This book . . . is not about definitions of prayer or termi-
> nology for prayer or arguments about prayer, though all of
> these have their place. Nor is it about methods and tech-
> niques of prayer, though I am sure we will discuss both.
> No, this book is about a love relationship: an enduring,
> continuing, growing love relationship with the great God

of the universe. And overwhelming love invites a response. Loving is the syntax of prayer. To be effective pray-ers, we need to be effective lovers . . . real prayer comes not from gritting our teeth but falling in love (*Prayer: Finding the Heart's True Home,* Harper San Francisco, 1992).

The teenage years are a season of life characterized by passion. When that passion is misused or misdirected, the results can be disastrous. When it is harnessed and directed by the Holy Spirit, the results can be explosive, life-changing, and world-impacting. A passionate, fired-up youth group can transform a local church. A cadre of passionate praying kids can transform a public high school. An auditorium or stadium full of passionately worshiping and praying young people can help transform a city, a region, or even a nation.

So how do we harness that prayer potential? How do we direct the passion of youth so that passionate praying and passionate pray-ers are the result? How do we disciple the emerging generations to cultivate their own intimacy with Christ and to storm heaven for the sake of the Kingdom of God and the fulfillment of the Great Commission? I believe three important ways we can do so are 1) modeling a lifestyle of prayer; 2) intentionally mentoring in prayer; and 3) mobilizing prayer initiatives.

Modeling a Lifestyle of Prayer

In my teens and early 20s, I had a short run as a competitive amateur golfer. In retrospect, what was likely obvious to others became so to me: my golfing style—swing, mannerisms, on-course disposition, putting style—was very much like that of my very skilled golfing father. Since he was the one who put a sawed-off golf club in my hand at age 18 months, and since I caddied for or played with him hundreds of times over the years, his influence was obviously profound. As he liked to say, "The apple doesn't fall far from the tree."

Prayer, along with a number of other spiritual disciplines, is like that: better caught than taught. Certainly, Jesus taught His followers about prayer (Mt. 6:3-15; Lk. 18:1-8), but even more so, He modeled prayer for them (Lk. 5:16; 6:12; 9:28ff; 11:1ff; 22:31-32, 39-46). I have many books on prayer in my library, but exposure over the years to the prayer habits of a relatively small number of prayer warriors (a few you would recognize, but most you would not) shaped my own praying more than a library of books. As a brand-new Christian, I learned to pray through the modeling of a small group of guys in my college fraternity. As a youth pastor in training, I learned to pray by intentionally hanging around a few leaders I knew who "had the goods" when it came to prayer. And as a budding prayer mobilizer and ministry leader, I sought out veteran prayer leaders, watched them in action, and then bought them coffee or meals while I peppered them with questions. Their answers, and examples, were invaluable.

To summarize: youth worker, the most significant influence you can have on the emerging generations when it comes to prayer is to model a lifestyle of prayer. This makes complete sense when we read what Paul has to say about modeling a lifestyle of discipleship; his comments can certainly apply to prayer:

Even though you have ten thousand guardians in Christ, you do not have many fathers, for in Christ Jesus I became your father through the gospel. Therefore, I urge you to imitate me. (1 Cor. 4:15)

Follow my example, as I follow the example of Christ. (11:1)

Remember your leaders, who spoke the word of God to you. Consider the outcome of their way of life and imitate their faith. (Heb. 13:7)

Mentoring in Prayer

Modeling with intentionality becomes mentoring. Mentoring is modeling on steroids. It's also the word we tend to use these days for discipleship, the biblical concept of investing in and imparting to others. Jesus modeled a lifestyle of prayer for all to see, but He was much more intentional with His followers (who were, by the way, called disciples, not mentees), mixing teaching and training in with His modeling.

Mentoring can be a two-edged sword. One of the first guys I mentored—and I use that term very loosely here—as a youth worker was Jack. We shared an interest in fishing, so in addition to connecting at youth activities, we spent a fair amount of time around rivers. Over time, I noticed that Jack began to imitate me—or should I say, he began to mimic some of my less-than-desirable characteristics and mannerisms. On one fishing excursion, Jack caught a female steelhead. While cleaning the fish, he took a handful of raw fish eggs and, mimicking his goofball youth pastor's joking behavior, turned to me and said, "Look, caviar!" and took a big bite. That didn't go well for Jack, and it was a sobering lesson for me as well.

In the next few pages, you are not going to get the latest, greatest programs for turning your students into prayer warriors. However, what you will get are resources for your proverbial prayer toolbox, and some direction where to find resources to better stock that toolbox. Tools are only as effective as the skillfulness of the one using them. Ask the Holy Spirit to show you which tools will work for your kids and ministry.

If you're led to use specific tools, be sure you're personally practicing them. All the tools/methods won't work for you. Some simply won't connect with your kids. Others might not be appropriate for your church culture. In other words, ask before taking the hedge trimmers and turning your church garden into a prayer labyrinth. Additionally, you likely own prayer tools not discussed here, methods already effective with your kids.

The late Lee Brase served as the prayer ministry coordinator for The Navigators for years, and mentored many people, young and old, in prayer. Including me. He offered five suggestions (in bold, followed by my comments) in the area of prayer mentoring:

> **Use Scripture.** Brase believed the most effective mentoring introduces people to biblical prayers. God recorded prayers in Scripture for many needs and feelings: frustration, grief, inner healing, joy, pain, praise, thanks, warfare, and more.
>
> **It's difficult but necessary to "unlearn" bad habits.** These habits can incorporate praying about surface issues rather than the underying issues; lengthy, wordy prayer rather than simply getting to the point; prayers directed to the people in the room rather than to God; prayers focusing primarily on asking rather than devotion and praise; praying from our viewpoint rather than seeking to pray from God's perspective.
>
> **Prayer works because of the volume of faith, not the volume of prayer.** God is not hard of hearing.
>
> **Praying people and the prayers of the Bible should be our mentors.**
>
> **Asking is the easy part of prayer; knowing what to ask is the difficult part.** (Adapted from Lee Brase, "The Word on Mentoring," *Pray!*, Mar/Apr 2000)

Veteran intercessor Candy Abbott provides some additional tips on mentoring:

> **Be patient.** Lead, but don't push. Let the student progress at the Holy Spirit's prompting.
>
> **Encourage your student to increase** while you decrease. That is, resist the urge to take over. Let the person do whatever he or she feels willing and able to do.

Pray often with and for the person you're mentoring.

Prepare for an investment in time and emotion. Be aware
that, as a bond of trust develops, your pupil will open
up to you and share innermost feelings. (Adapted from
Canby Abbott, "Tips on Mentoring," *Pray!*, Mar/
Apr 2000).

In my mentoring experience, I've identified two common fears
among students. First, the fear of praying out loud. Many students
(and adults) get intimidated by praying aloud. The reasons are
varied, the most prominent being lack of confidence. It's helpful
to encourage students gradually. A good place to start is to give
them a simple sentence prayer to finish, such as "I praise You, God,
because You are . . ." Or, "Thank you, Lord, for . . ." Encourage
their successes. Remind them God is more concerned about the
attitude of the heart than the adequacy of vocabulary.

Accordingly, don't place students in a position where they
need to pray out loud in a group setting, unless you know they
have some measure of experience and/or comfort in doing so. The
resulting embarrassment for them is counterproductive to prayer
mentoring. Encourage students to pray out loud during their
personal devotional times. This also helps them stay focused while
praying. And be sure they hear you pray out loud often.

A second common fear for new pray-ers is not knowing what
to pray. To elaborate on Brace's suggestion 4 above: While it is
true that praying people and the prayers of the Bible should be our
mentors, praying people who pray the prayers of the Bible are our
best mentors! When it comes to prayers of the Bible, the best place
to start is Psalms. Dietrich Bonhoeffer writes, "Now there is in the
Holy Scriptures a book which is distinguished from all other books
of the Bible by the fact that it contains only prayer. The book is the
Psalms" (Bonhoeffer, *Psalms: The Prayer Book of the Bible*, Broadleaf
Books 2022, pg. 13).

Obviously, The Lord's Prayer is a big deal here as well, as it is Jesus' response to the request of His disciples, "Lord, teach us to pray." (Luke 11:1).

Additionally, there are many other prayers in the Bible that can serves as templates for our own praying. Here are a few examples:

- Paul prayed for the Philippians: "And this is my prayer: that your love may abound more and more in knowledge and depth of insight, so that you may be able to discern what is best and may be pure and blameless until the day of Christ, filled with the fruit of righteousness that comes through Jesus Christ—to the glory and praise of God." (Phil. 1:9-11) His prayers for the Romans (Rom. 15:5-6, 13), Ephesians (Eph. 1:15-19; 3:14-19), Colossians (Col. 1:9-12), and Thessalonians (1 Thess. 3:11-13; 2 Thess. 1:11-12) are also excellent model prayers.
- Paul asked for prayer from the Ephesians: "Pray also for me, that whenever I open my mouth, words may be given me so that I will fearlessly make known the mystery of the gospel . . . pray that I may declare it fearlessly, as I should." (Eph. 6:19-20) A very similar prayer is found in Colossians 4:3-4.

Mentoring comes into pray here as we help students take these model prayers and adapt them for use today in their own lives and situations.

Mobilizing Prayer Initiatives

An addition to modeling a lifestyle of prayer and intentionally mentoring in prayer, mobilizing prayer initiatives introduces a group dynamic to the whole creating a culture of prayer enterprise.

Example: at one of the churches where I served as youth pastor, we launched the Epaphras Wrestling Club, taken from Colossians 4:12: "Epaphras, who is one of you and a servant of Christ Jesus, sends greetings. He is always wrestling in prayer for you, that you may stand firm in all the will of God, mature and fully assured." We printed up T shirts (with some lame wrestling graphic), stickers, membership cards, and more, all to get students praying for each other. I'm not remembering that the shelf life of that initiative was very long, but we had fun with it for a season.

Here are some other ideas that may be helpful. Just remember, it is important to seek the Lord for initiatives that will work with your youth group in your church in your culture. An Epaphras Wrestling Club idea may get laughed at and/or mocked into the "not for us" file.

> **Sitting in His Presence**. We're working with a generation that's not comfortable with, and even can fear, silence. Encouraging students to simply "be with" God in silence and solitude—both individually, and in curated corporate environments during youth nights or on a retreat—can build a prayer breakthrough for them. But it could take time for students to reach this point.
>
> **Acronyms**. These outline a reliable path to help kids learn to pray. One of the most popular acronyms for a prayer method is ACTS: adoration, confession, thanksgiving, and supplication. Another is PRAY: praise, repent, ask, yield. Create your own acronym, if you prefer. Acronyms suggest the content so students don't wonder what to pray about.
>
> **Prayer Lists and Journals**. Many pray-ers use these, but few employ them well. The more elaborately structured the lists and/or journals, the more difficult it becomes for youth to use them consistently over the long run.

A prayer journal can create room for a list that records requests so learners can pray in an orderly and consistent manner. The list can leave room for recording God's faithfulness through answered prayer. The journal can also provide space for students to write out their prayers. Many find this beneficial because it helps them stay focused. Try to find a prayer journal with a simple learning curve, or custom-make journals for or with your students. In one of my youth groups, we had these cool faux leather covers made, with our ministry logo on the front, with a custom journal inside.

Prayer and Worship Retreats. My friend Wayne had attended a youth worker Prayer Summit I facilitated, and now he was on the phone, asking me to fly across the country to lead a similar event for his youth group. We would start on Friday night, finish with lunch on Sunday, and our agenda consisted of prayer. That was it: no mixers, no speakers, and no wild outdoor games. The kids knew they were signing up for a "prayer retreat," but they had no clue how literally that would be taken. I took the assignment with a bit of trepidation, which the students validated when we arrived at the venue and Wayne briefed them. I observed a lot of big eyes and open mouths. "We're going to do what?"

But guess what? We made it. Kids who'd never prayed continuously for more than a half hour were completely stoked that they had prayed in a number of creative ways—and worshiped, because it's often hard to separate the two—for an entire weekend. The point is: youth can do this. And it will have a bigger impact on their lives than a lowest common denominator "Kumbaya Klub" retreat ever could.

Prayerwalking. For students (and youth leaders) who struggle with sitting still, or snoozing while praying, prayerwalking—which is simply praying while you walk, or as Steve Hawthorne describes it, "praying on-site with insight"—helps one stay focused while praying, and to visually connect with the object of one's prayers. Prayerwalks can be done alone or in groups, around the perimeter of schools (sometimes called "Jericho Walks"), through halls, or in neighborhoods.

They can also be quite creative. In one small community, a youth group met at five a.m. at a different school each week, driving inconspicuous stakes into the ground, with relevant Scripture written on them, at each corner of the school grounds. The students strategically prayerwalked the hallways during school hours. A Christian teacher periodically invited local youth workers into the classroom while the students left for lunch. With heads up and eyes open to look less conspicuous, they interceded for students, teachers and the school before prayerwalking the halls on the way out.

Holy Ground and Prayer Apps. These seem to be multiplying so rapidly that any list I generate here will be outdated by the time this book hits the market. So I would like to focus on one: Holy Ground is a prayerwalking app developed by 24-7 Prayer USA and Civil Righteousness that uses GPS to track exactly where you've walked. If your youth group is motivated/inspired to prayerwalk all the neighborhoods surrounding their church or the area schools, participants log into the app when they begin, and it will track, with a red line, every road or space where students have walked while praying. How cool is that!

Like I said, are many more prayer apps available—Inner Room and Lectio 365 seem to be quite popular at the moment—and of course the Claim Your Campus app, but as is the case with apps in general, you'll need to "try them on" to see which ones fit you, your students, and your ministry.

Contemplative Resources. Centering prayer, meditation, and sacred reading appear among the prayer forms practiced by Catholics, Episcopalians, Orthodox, and mainline denominational believers for centuries. The broader Church is rediscovering the value of these practices. Prayer labyrinths are showing up at youth conferences. Prayer icons are appearing on the walls of youth rooms. The ancient Jesus Prayer and centering prayer are infiltrating evangelical circles. This is a very good thing! Many of these practices may be new to you, so take time to learn about them. It will be worth it to your kids, and to you as well.

An additional thing to remember when using these or any other prayer tools is the widely accepted educational theory asserting that the more "gates" (sensory portals of hearing, seeing, speaking, smelling, and touching) used to impart information, the better that information will be received and utilized. Think: students *hearing* you and others pray—even with your eyes open! *Seeing* others pray communicates that it's "legit" to pray, or be in the presence of praying people, even with your eyes open. Often prayer's facial and body expressions instruct: bowed heads or uplifted hands or bended knees. Students can *speak* aloud their own prayers, *holding* the Scriptures or a prayer book in their hands as they pray (or if they are Catholic, handle the prayer beads of a rosary). *Smelling* incense in a place of prayer can also stimulate pray-ers.

Fanning the Flame

Once upon a time, God showed up at one of my summer camps. His presence was palpable and shook us all. We worshiped and prayed for hours. Almost everyone there who was not saved got saved, and we were up for most of the last night, unable to sleep. Many of those kids returned home changed. Sadly, the change was short-lived for some and the cause, at least in part, was a "fan failure" on my part. Paul exhorted Timothy to "fan into flame the gift of God" (2 Tim. 1:6). When I had a bunch of kids who were ready to receive some serious fanning, I wasn't sure how to do that. (I hadn't read this book yet!)

When students look like they might be "getting" prayer—as a result of a unique experience, mentoring, or God turning their hearts towards Him by some other means—we need to encourage them as best we can, playing our part as shepherds in the fanning process. All students need a periodic fanning related to prayer, but when we identify those who are F.A.T. (faithful, available, and teachable) kids, they warrant more focused attention. That is true mentoring or discipling. Jesus fanned His disciples with a gentle breeze, used a stronger wind with His apostles, and let loose a hurricane on James, John, and Peter. Who knows? Perhaps some of the fanned kids in our groups will be the prayer warriors of tomorrow!

Chapter 9

Prayer for Big and Special Events

When we work, we work. When we pray, God works.

—J. Hudson Taylor

I WAS IN WAY over my head and I knew it. Sure, I had organized prayer support for some of our youth group's outreaches, and I'd led small teams of intercessors in prayer during the evangelistic youth rallies that accompanied a 1992 Billy Graham Crusade in Portland, Oregon. But this was taking prayer support to a new level: a total of 10 days of on-site prayer coverage for 30,000 students attending Youth for Christ's two Youth Evangelism Super Conferences in Washington, D.C., and Los Angeles, California. I knew I needed help . . . and fast!

It started innocently enough. I taught at a YFC regional conference on the importance of prayer in youth ministry. One conversation led to another, and before I knew it, I committed to mobilizing and deploying on-site prayer support for two gigantic youth events. So, I started making calls for help.

Chuck Pierce is today one of the leaders of the global prayer movement and a prolific author on a variety of prayer-related subjects. In in 1994, Chuck was an emerging leader who agreed to join me in D.C. to teach me the ropes of on-site prayer. Chuck was the point person for our team of about a dozen people recruited from all over the United States. For the most part, I played the part of eager learner, taking in everything I could. We arrived the day before the conference began. Under Chuck's leadership, we engaged in a prayerwalk of the conference venue, spiritual warfare prayer in the convention hall and meeting rooms, and worship and intercession in an assigned prayer room.

Once the students arrived, we continued with the same pattern for about 10 hours a day. I still played the part of eager learner until day three, when Chuck informed me he had another commitment in the D.C. area and I would lead our prayer team that morning. With much trepidation, I sent a few from our team to pray in various venues, and stayed with a group of about 10 in our prayer room. Things seemed to go well until the entire group started praying in their "prayer languages." Loudly. For a very long time. And so, being the strong, discerning leader I was, I quit and went home. Well, not really, but at the time I sure wished Chuck was there!

With Chuck's help I made it through that week. Since then, I've led on-site prayer teams for quite a few big events—a half-dozen DC/LA conferences; the Atlanta '96 Youth Worker Conference; a number of Youth Specialties conventions; some National Network of Youth Ministries Forums; plus, a variety of local, regional, and national student gatherings.

My experience in D.C. in '94 was just the tip of the iceberg when it relates to surprising experiences with prayer teams. At one venue, a team member stood at the window of our prayer room that overlooked the auditorium and started honking loudly. When I asked him what he was doing, he replied he had the gift of being a human *shofar* (a ram's horn used in the Old Testament for either a call to worship or battle) and was exercising his gift. In another venue, we had a mutiny of sorts on our prayer team. A few members felt we needed to proceed in a different direction from our present course, and eventually left to go their own way in a different room. Now *that* gave the conference leadership a lot of confidence in what we were doing!

I've got numerous war stories: some humorous, some definitely not. But for every unusual story, I have many more stories of God working in and through our on-site teams in ways that significantly enhanced the spiritual impact of many events. Back to DC/LA '94: 20,000 students had gathered at the Capitol Mall for a culminating rally and the weather report was not good. Thunderstorms were forecast for the area, and we could see them fast approaching. Canceling the rally was a serious possibility, given the imminent danger of lightning strikes. Standing behind the stage, the DC/LA leadership briefed us about the weather. Then Chuck Pierce deployed us: some prayerwalking the venue; others standing in a corner, hands raised against the approaching thunderheads, agreeing in prayer God would move the storm. In a clearly supernatural experience, the approaching clouds did a 180-degree turn, headed the other way, and the rally commenced! This caught the attention of the DC/LA leadership in a profound way, and was the seminal event in transforming DC/LA prayer support from an experiment to an integral part of their ongoing strategy.

Stories like this fit into the category of "really cool." But the many incidents of prayer teams watching what they prayed "in secret" birthed in arenas among students, fall into the "really, really cool" category for sure. The unity of folks from around the country, who didn't know each other well, coming together to pray God's desires into reality is nothing short of amazing. It's those stories that authenticate and validate the importance of prayer support for strategic big and special events.

Why Big and Special Events?

During my early years as a youth pastor in a small town, our church led an attractional program called "Son City." Every week was a "big event," with competition, drama, live music, multimedia presentations, compelling messages, and a whole lot of energy.

Students with much more time on their hands than today would show up on Wednesday nights and linger well after we shut down the music. We would throw a Burger Bash and 25 percent of the student population of the town would show up. That style of ministry, and the accompanying attendance, is the exception rather than the norm in this season and this culture. But big and special events are still of the utmost importance.

Most of us are aware that the optimal context for spiritual change is relationships. As youth workers, the greatest long-term impact we will have with students is in the context of relational and incarnational interaction, be it on a school campus, in a coffee shop, on a river (don't eat the eggs!) or at a youth group gathering. However, the big and special events of our ministries—camps, conferences, missions trips, rallies, retreats—remain "booster rockets" that propel students far ahead in their spiritual pilgrimages in a short period of time. Major personal decisions are often made at big events, whether they are decisions to follow Christ, commitments to personal holiness; decisions to stay sexually pure; or choices to pursue careers in ministry or missions. Although these decisions must be verified and solidified in the context of relationships, discipleship, and daily living, they are nevertheless vital and often life-changing choices. As youth workers, we want to do all we can to make these big events as significant and life-changing as possible. Which is why we pray.

The goal of any big event strategy is to help create an environment, through prayer, that will produce maximum spiritual impact in the lives of a maximum number of students. Certainly, prayer for the more tangible elements of big events—the location, cost, location, music, program, speaker, worship, activities—is very important. A poorly staged big event that does not capture the imagination of students presents a challenge when it comes to creating an environment of spiritual impact through prayer. On the other hand, a high-quality event with all the bells and whistles but little or no prayer strategy is no better. I've seen mediocre events in terms of structure and content, but because background people bathed them in concerted prayer, the spiritual impact upon those in attendance was significant. In contrast, I've seen events that featured high profile speakers and musicians, a multitude of audiovisual delights, and enough fog machines to shut down an airport; yet the impact on students' lives was minimal. Prayer was sacrificed on the altar of programming.

Big and special events differ greatly in their purpose and content, and prayer strategy particulars also differ from venue to venue. However, the governing principles that determine the strategy remain relatively constant. The rest of this chapter addresses the scenario of a youth leader preparing to bring students to a big event staged by someone else, although the principles also apply to a self-staged small event. For you and your ministry, that could be a dozen kids going to a mountain cabin for a weekend, which is great! Get the prayer going! The following three principles still apply: 1) a biblical, historical, and cultural perspective; 2) the priority of prayer support; and 3) particulars of formulating a prayer strategy.

A Healthy Perspective

Too often, we youth workers tend to go about our planning, and tack prayer on as an addendum. I know, I've already covered this at length earlier, but it bears repeating: we make our plans and then ask God to bless them, rather than asking God to give us the plans and bless their implementation. Most of us realize how important prayer is. Then why don't we pray more? And why don't we make prayer the integral part of our preparations? I've found taking the time to gain a healthy perspective helps.

In the initial stages of developing a big event prayer strategy, it helps to recount the biblical, historical, and cultural perspectives of prayer. Again, I am repeating myself, but maybe the repetition will help this stuff sink in: "If two of you on earth agree about anything you ask for, it will be done for you by my Father in heaven" (Mt. 18:19); "If you believe, you will receive whatever you ask for in prayer" (Mt. 21:22); "Apart from me you can do nothing" (Jn. 15:5); "But in everything, by prayer and petition, with thanksgiving, present your requests to God" (Phil. 4:6).

I have found it more than helpful to go back over these "standard" passages on the priority of prayer and meditate on them until they seep into the inner recesses of my soul. It's also motivating and convicting to study biblical characters like Nehemiah, Jehoshaphat, or Daniel, who won battles (certainly big events!) and impacted nations through prayer. Such meditations and studies help narrow the gap between what we know in our heads and hearts about prayer, and what we practice on a daily basis in our lives and ministries.

Biographies help, too: the men and women used by God to shape lives and shake the world are, almost always, men and women of prayer. Often, they spent hours on their knees each morning before the workday started. Too often, we take a group of students to a big or special event that could change lives, with only a minimal amount of prayer support invested before or during it.

The Prayer Priority

Organizing an event or a trip to someone else's event can be a daunting task. There are students to motivate and sign up, money to raise, travel plans to make, adult sponsors to recruit, lodging to secure—all critical to the success of a trip. A problem comes when we allow the tasks to consume our time and energies to the detriment of mobilizing prayer support from church members, parents, and the students themselves.

When we fall into this trap (and most of us do at one time or another), it's time to stop, regain perspective, and re-visit what our priority should be. Remember: the goal of a big-event prayer strategy is to help create an environment, through prayer, that will produce maximum spiritual impact in the lives of a maximum number of students. That type of environment is created not primarily through greater attendance, or better funding, or a classier retreat facility—but primarily *through prayer*.

Prayer Strategy Particulars

A healthy perspective about mobilizing prayer support for big events, and a commitment to make prayer a top priority, must be followed by the practicality of prayer strategy particulars. Prayer is not a theory, it is a practice, and the practice should be both well thought through and do-able.

I have mobilized prayer support for big events when I was the guy running the event (which can be exhausting). I have also mobilized prayer for a variety of local, regional, and national big events, and served as an intercessor for many others. In each case, the strategy differed, depending on the style of the event, the pool of humanity from which to draw prayer support, and the creativity of the prayer mobilizers. In a local church setting, there are three strategic components of that pool of humanity to target when mobilizing prayer: parishioners, parents, and participants. Try these ideas for mobilizing an event:

Praying Parishioners

Encourage members of your congregation to adopt a student for focused prayer before, during, and after the big event. Take digital photos of participating students and staff, and create prayer I.D. cards listing relevant prayer issues at the bottom. This will give intercessors a visible prayer reminder they can stick in their Bible or on the refrigerator.

Set up a prayer clock during the event. Members of your congregation can sign up to intercede for your students and the event during set times each day. This could be 24 hours around the clock or whatever works best for you. For a visual reminder, make a large poster showing a clock broken down into fifteen-minute segments, with intercessors' names written in, and post it in the church fellowship hall or another visible location.

Develop a prayer chain within your church. During the big event, call in current and pressing prayer concerns at regular intervals for quick prayer responses.

Utilize bulletin inserts or slides during announcement time in services, for mobilizing prayer. List those who will be attending, relevant prayer issues, who to contact for involvement in the adoption ministry or prayer clock, and so on.

Identify and mobilize prayer groups and individual intercessors to cover your group and the event in prayer. Senior citizens seem to have a special affinity for youth and love to pray for them. This is an excellent way to involve them in youth ministry.

Challenge folks in your congregation to come with you to the event with the express purpose of interceding for your group and other aspects of the event.

Praying Parents

Take the time to explain to parents your desires for the event and for their kids. Let them know it's not only a fun excursion, but also a potentially life-changing experience. Let them know that prayers for the event, and for those attending, are critical to its success. Because they are.

Teach parents how to pray more effectively for their children—both during the event, and ongoing. Moms In Prayer and other ministries provide excellent resources in this area.

Give them specific prayer points to guide their intercession before, during, and after the event.

Affirm to them your commitment to pray for their children, and let them know you value their input and interaction as you partner in prayer.

Praying Participants

Make prayer a requirement for Christian students attending the big event, as well as for their adult sponsors. Ask them to make a commitment to pray regularly for various aspects of the event: musicians, programming leaders, speakers, students who will attend, unsaved students, and so on.

Divide students into prayer triplets that meet on a regular basis before, during, and after the event. In these smaller groups, more-detailed prayer requests can be shared and focused on.

Make united prayer a top priority in your preparatory time together.

Train adult sponsors in prayer. Assign students to each adult for focused prayer. Teach them how to pray "on site with insight." (i.e. pray continually while allowing the unfolding dynamics of the event itself to shape prayers). Integrate united prayer into your sponsor briefings.

Model a lifestyle of prayer. Show students, adult sponsors, and others in your congregation you are serious about making prayer foundational in this big event and your youth ministry in general.

These ideas represent just the tip of the iceberg when it comes to creative ideas for mobilizing prayer. Let your imagination soar and allow the Holy Spirit to be your guide. Remember: your goal is to help create an environment, through prayer, that will produce maximum spiritual impact in the lives of a maximum number of students. With a prayer strategy in place, big events can reap tremendous fruit. And when a prayer strategy becomes foundational in your ministry, fruitfulness will continue. The lives of many of your students will never be the same!

Postscript: On-Site Prayer Team Guidelines

Below are guidelines I have used with a variety of on-site prayer teams. They help ensure all your team members are "on the same page" when you engage in intercession. You can adjust them to fit your situation and needs, as I have. Because there is "nothing new under the sun" (Ecc. 1:9), I'm sure I borrowed from others who have gone before me. I just don't know what, and from whom!

1. Preparation for the event.
    A. Check your armor (Eph. 6:10-17).
    B. Check your character and relationships.
        1. Humility (2 Chron. 7:14, 20:12).
        2. Compassion and empathy (Mt. 9:35-38).
        3. Submission (Jas. 4:7).
        4. Personal sin issues (Ps. 66:18; Is. 59:2).
        5. Marriage and family life (1 Pet. 3:7).
        6. Other relationships (Jn. 13:34-35, 14:15-21, 17:20-23; 1 Tim. 2:8).
    C. Check your motives (1 Chron. 28:9; Prov. 16:2; 1 Cor. 4:5; Jas. 4:3).

2. Participation in united prayer sessions.
    A. Invite His presence (2 Chron. 20:21-22; Josh. 6).
    B. Request His protection (Deut. 23:14; Ps. 5:11, 32:7; John 17:11, 15; 2 Thess. 3:3)
    C. Appropriate His power. Silence the enemy; subdue his influence (Mt. 10:1).
    D. Plead His promises. Use the Word of God—there are promises in abundance!
    E. Seek His purposes.

1. Be about seeking and inquiring (Zeph.1:6; Josh. 9:14)

2. Flow with the Spirit (Rom. 8:26). A key to effective intercession is allowing the Holy Spirit to conform your prayers to the will of God—discerning the mind of Christ concerning what to pray, where to pray, when to pray. That requires much listening as well as speaking. Don't be afraid of silence.

3. Positioning the prayer team.

   A. Each member has a role/function on the team. (1 Cor. 12).

   1. Everyone is important!

   2. If you're a "foot" don't try to be a "hand."

   B. Submission to leadership is critical to the proper functioning of the team.

   C. On-site prayer means more than gathering in a room. Include plenty of prayer walking, praying within general sessions, praying through room accommodations, and more.

   D. Be inclusive. Don't pray through general sessions or rallies while forgetting seminars, breakout sessions, and other places.

4. Persevering through the event.

   A. Be persistent (Lk. 11:5-13; 18:1-5).

   B. Pace yourself. Intercessors can burn out from long hours and little sleep just like, event leaders and sponsors/counselors.

Chapter 10

Praying for the Campus, Community and City

*There is nothing that makes us love a man so much
as praying for him.*

—WILLIAM LAW

*Light yourself on fire with passion and people will come
from miles to watch you burn.*

—JOHN WESLEY

WHILE MY transition into vocational youth ministry was unorthodox, the gift of hindsight helps it make sense. I was raised Mormon, left that at age 13, and started attending Young Life meetings while in high school. I had close to zero spiritual interest at the time, and 100 percent of my motivation was sourced in the girls who attended the weekly club meetings. But the leader showed an interest in me, showed up at my athletic events, let me occasionally play back-up guitar, and even asked if I could host a Young Life Club meeting at my home. We developed a friendship, so when the invitation came to attend a weekend retreat, there was no hesitation on my part. That weekend, I heard the Gospel for the first time, and placed my trust in Christ. Statistics tell us that most people who come to Christ do so before age 20, so I was a stat.

Statistics also say that most people become hair-on-fire-for-Jesus during their college years. I was a stat for that, too. If you've seen the movie *Jesus Revolution*, I was a product of that movement. We had a mini-revival on my college campus, and in particular, my fraternity. I transformed from party animal on academic probation to fraternity chaplain on the honor roll in the span of a few months.

When my church asked me to bring my goofball guitar-playing schtick on staff as a vocational youth worker, my response was a no-brainer. My passion for Jesus was ignited during my college years, but ignition would not have taken place without meeting Christ during my high school years. Consequently, the example of my Young Life leader became the template for my entrance into vocational youth ministry.

During my agnostic years in high school, I'm not sure that many of my Christian classmates were mission or missionary-driven. Back in the day, that tended to happen during the college years. That is not the case today! In the midst of the cultural insanities in which many adolescents are just trying to survive rather than thrive, there are a growing number of high school students, even junior highers, who are lit for Jesus and on mission with Him. I will call them The Remnant for now because they're relatively small in number, but possess a large, even fierce, faith. These activists whose passion for Jesus is paired with a passion for reaching their campuses, communities, country, and even the nations of the world. You are noticing them in your ministries, aren't you? We have the privilege of helping to prepare and deploy them on a lifetime of missional living, which starts now.

No matter what vocational direction the Lord leads The Remnant to pursue, teaching them that their prayers in the here-and-now can touch, impact, and change the world around them is huge. In the next pages, I've listed a few ways to do this. But to repeat an earlier disclaimer: the ministry landscape, often (but not always) reflected online, is evolving at an ever-faster rate. Today's websites are sometimes tomorrow's stale information sites. Between the time when my fingers hit the keyboard and this book hits the market, what is hot could be not. So take my recommendations and suggestions as a starting point for your own research.

See You at the Pole (www.syatp.com)

Many of us have heard of—and likely been involved with—See You at the Pole, a movement established by students who gather to pray at their school flagpoles at 7 a.m. on the third Wednesday of September each year. Beginning in 1990 with a small group of Texas teenagers, the idea of standing together in prayer for their schools resonated powerfully with students nationally and internationally, and the movement exploded to involve literally millions worldwide. Over 30 years later, while the numbers may not match those of the early years, SYATP still assembles as a catalytic event in many parts of the country.

Claim Your Campus (www.claimyourcampus.org)

This prayer movement is a "big deal," and it's getting bigger. Unless you skipped the second Selah section (no!), you read about it in the article by Olivia Williamson.

Campus Alliance (www.everyschool.com)

The Campus Alliance is a coalition of more than 30 national youth-ministry denominations and organizations united to reach every middle school, junior high, and high school in America. It utilizes a prayer, care, and share strategy. This group shares many student and campus-oriented prayer strategies and resources on its website.

Tenx10 (www.tenx10.org)

Tenx10 (pronounced ten by ten) is a very broad ecumenical collaboration involving close to 100 youth ministry organizations and denominations, with four strategic priorities: 1) Helping faith matter more to 10 million young people over the next 10 years.

2) Offering the resources faith communities need to prioritize youth discipleship. 3) Sparking an ecumenical movement that supports and equips youth leaders on the frontlines of cultivating the faith of the next generation. 4) Seeing and centering leaders in communities of color as well as bi-vocational, volunteer, and under-resourced leaders. Their website was being populated as of this writing, but good prayer resources are sure to be there.

Other Prayer Ideas

Aside from joining or drawing from organized groups, these ideas can prompt prayer inside and outside a campus:

Yearbooks. Students can scan every picture and name from a school yearbook (after getting permission from the school, of course), place them on cards with relevant information, and list ways to pray. Distribute them to people who will pray regularly for one or more students.

Lockers. Ask Christian students to pray for peers with lockers in close proximity to their own. For instance, pray for students with five lockers to the right and five lockers to the left. Pray for whatever number works to cover all the lockers.

Home Room. At some schools, each student attends a short "home room" at the beginning of the school day. The Christians in each home room can take on the rest of the students as their prayer assignment. While in the home room, they pray for the other students.

Station Banners. As a high school student in Wichita, Kansas, Brandon ignited with a passion for prayer at a summer prayer conference his family attended. The Lord stirred him with a vision to pray for his school. With little knowledge of how to proceed, Brandon gathered a few friends and started meeting weekly to pray. He and a friend created banners to guide their prayers and keep them focused. The banners described four prayer station themes:

- Station One: The Lost. Pray God will save the lost (2 Pet. 3:9).
- Station Two: Leaders. Pray God will move in the lives of teachers and administration (1 Tim. 3:1-2).
- Station Three: Strongholds. Pray God will break strongholds in the school through spiritual warfare (2 Cor. 10:4). Ask God to reveal where Satan keeps control. When these strongholds are identified, pray He will break them and work freely in the school.
- Station Four: Revival. Pray God will send revival (Acts 2:17).

Moving from station to station at five-minute intervals, they wrote the names of classmates and teachers on the banners, praying for them by name.

God moved powerfully at Brandon's school, and this intrepid group of "banner pray-ers" grew rapidly. Christian students at other schools adopted this or similar methods as student prayer groups multiplied throughout Wichita and other cities in Kansas. A few years later, I stood next to Brandon as he cast a vision for campus prayer to more than 6,000 students at a national conference, and then led them in a powerful concert of prayer.

Prayerwalks. This was covered in an earlier chapter; I mention it again because it really seems to resonate with students!

Prayer Clocks. Recruit students, parents, teachers, and others to sign up and pray for your school. Every person would pray for a 10-minute stretch each school day. If you recruit 96 people to pray, people pray for your school continuously from 6:00 a.m. until 10:00 p.m. every school day. If that seems daunting, get enough people to pray bell-to-bell: from the start of school to dismissal.

30-Second Kneel Downs. This prayer evangelism strategy consists of students kneeling down at their schools, in front of their lockers or in another public venue, on a daily basis for 30 seconds of focused prayer. The suggested time is 7:30 a.m. The purpose is 1) to broaden the school prayer base; 2) to put prayer back in school in a way that doesn't break the law; 3) to develop students' reputations as Christians so they can freely share the Gospel on campus. The time can break up into three segments:

> **Segment 1:** God, Thanks! "God, I bow my knee in humility to You. I know Your loving presence will be with me all day. Thank You for loving me today. I love You, too!" "Love the Lord your God with all your heart, with all your soul and with all your mind" (Mt. 22:37).
>
> **Segment 2:** God, Touch Them! "God, touch the teachers, administration, and students on my campus today. One touch from You, Father, can change someone's destiny. Touch them through me." "Love your neighbor as yourself" (vs. 39).
>
> **Segment 3:** God, Tell Them! "God, the message of Jesus' love for my campus must be told. Use me as the messenger. I will tell those around me how much You love them." "Therefore, go and make disciples of all nations" (28:19).

Prayer Lockers. A hallway locker can be designated as a "prayer locker" where students drop prayer requests through slits at the top of the door. Ask students who use the locker to also drop in notes when God answers their requests. Then mobilize Christian students to hit their knees! When God answers these prayers, students will feel blessed, and they might increase their spiritual interest. Note: be prepared for incoming stuff that is anything but prayer request worthy.

Prayer and Fasting. Many students learn to fast in conjunction with prayer. When Jesus' disciples tried to help a young person in spiritual bondage, they were powerless. Jesus told them, "This kind does not go out except by prayer and fasting" (Mt. 17:21, NASB). Students and faculty can fast by skipping breakfast and lunch on the first Friday of each month, and use that time for personal or corporate prayer for their campus.

Prayer Guides. Students often feel motivated to pray, but don't know what to say. A succinct prayer guide can be helpful, providing what to pray and the reasons behind the prayers. When mobilizing students to pray, don't assume anything or overwhelm them with too many prayer points.

Prayer Zone Partners for Adults. By law, yellow school zone signs appear on the roads surrounding public schools. They slow down the speed limits. Prayer Zone Partners use these signs to remind folks to pray for neighboring schools every time they drive through a school zone.

The concept of Prayer Zone Partners originated from David Mewbourne, Oklahoma district Youth Alive director. One day while David drove to work, he was late and stuck in a school zone. David slowed to the posted speed limit. As David complained to himself, God quickly reminded him of his personal commitment to schools, students, teachers, and campus ministry. God showed him that traveling through a school zone offered an excellent time to pray for that school. From that point on, David converted school zones into prayer zones.

As a reminder to pray, Zone Partners place yellow, diamond-shaped, static stickers in the corner of their windshields. The stickers can be customized to focus on an individual ministry, network, city movement, or specific school. "Change your oil, but don't change your prayer zone!"

Choose Your Own

I remind you again to ask the Holy Spirit to help you pick which
of these prayer tools will work for your ministry. You can also adapt
or adjust something I've suggested to make it even more effective
in your situation! I could continue with more examples of great
ideas and strategies to help young people pray for their community,
nation, and the world. But the Internet explodes with creative
ideas. Just use a good search engine to find the most current
resources. Let the surfing begin!

Chapter 11

Filling Up Bowls

The great people of the earth today are the people who
pray—not those who talk about prayer; nor those who say
they believe in prayer; nor those who can explain about
prayer; but those who take time to pray.

—S. D. GORDON

I HAVE GIVEN doctors permission to cut open my eyeballs. Twice.

Years ago, my wife convinced me to undergo LASIK laser eye surgery. I have a video of the procedure. They sliced the top off my eyeballs, shot a laser at my corneas, and flipped the top back on. After the humiliation of wearing thick black glasses in junior high to correct my myopia—the kind of glasses sold today with a moustache attached underneath—I wore contact lenses for decades until LASIK. Since then, freedom! No worrying about contact lenses, cases, solutions to pack around, or dry, itching eyes on long plane flights.

In college, I briefly played on the racquetball team, before eye protection was mandatory. Yup, I took a racquetball to the eye, temporarily lost sight in that eye, spent three days in the infirmary, but recovered nicely. Unfortunately, the injury caused the lens in my eye to slowly get cloudy, until it eventually needed replacement. So, recently they sliced my eye open again, sucked the old lens out, put in a new, fake one, which produced clear eyesight.

Myopia and Cloudy Vision

What in the world does my eye drama have to do with a praying youth ministry, you might be asking? In a sentence, myopia and cloudy vision. The American Heritage Dictionary (version 3.0.1 for Macintosh) defines myopia as "a visual defect in which distant objects appear blurred because their images are focused in front of the retina rather than on it. Nearsightedness. Also called short sight." LASIK surgery corrected my myopia, which the lens replacement surgery corrected my cloudy vision. Both myopia and cloudy vision are occupational hazards in youth ministry. Our ministry nearsightedness and cloudy vision keeps us focused on things like how the students liked our most recent message, or how many parents are mad at us, or how we can increase youth group attendance, or even how are we going to keep our job.

One of the advantages of being involved in youth ministry for over 45 years is perspective. I'm not as short-sighted as I used to be, nor is my vision as cloudy when it comes to the spiritual significance of what I am doing—or should I say, what we who are involved in this youth ministry calling are doing. Yes, there was a season when then the youth worker was the defacto second hire at most churches, when 500 kids would show up at a poorly pro-moted Burger Bash, and successful church plants would grow out of thriving youth ministries. But that is no longer the case.

The number of vocational youth workers has dropped precipi-tously, and they are the fourth or even fifth hire. Five hundred kids choose other things to occupy their time - like curating their social media outlets - than showing up at a Burger Bash. Church plants no longer grow out of youth ministry, but are now often started by ex-youth pastors so frustrated by the craziness of contemporary youth culture and contemporary youth ministry that they figure church planting (or the secular marketplace) is an easier gig. While youth workers used to thrive, now they survive.

My point in the above is not to disparage youth ministry; I think I made that clear earlier in the book. Statistically, adolescence still represents the best season for people to come to Christ. The discipling of youth—to solidify decisions made in pre-adolescence—remains an urgent priority. Many prophetic and intercessory types sense college *and* secondary school campuses will be seedbeds for the next major spiritual awaking in America. I agree.

There are a few fascinating passages in the book of Revelation that present a healthy correction to our youth ministry myopia and cloudy vision:

> And when he had taken it, the four living creatures and the twenty-four elders fell down before the Lamb. Each one had a harp and they were holding golden bowls full of incense, which are the prayers of the saints. (5:8)

> Another angel, who had a golden censer, came and stood at the altar. He was given much incense to offer, with the prayers of all the saints, on the golden altar before the throne. The smoke of the incense, together with the prayers of the saints, went up before God from the angel's hand. (8:3-4)

Filling Up Bowls

I confess that I do not have a firm grip on much of the prophetic metaphor and imagery of Revelation. This is certainly true regarding golden bowls of incense and the prayers of the saints. But God used these verses to correct my myopic, cloudy vision to a degree. I realized that our prayers—large and small, lengthy and short, articulate and unspoken, passionate and perfunctory—are coming together in some profoundly spiritual way that is beyond our understanding. They please God as a fragrant offering, and they release His purposes on the earth. Heavenly bowls are being filled with the prayers of intercessors both great and small, young and old, male and female, from every nation—youth workers and others!

I have a feeling that the bowl-filling capacity of a prayer, or prayers, is not measured by our criteria. We *all* contribute to filling up the bowls, as have believers who have offered up prayers throughout history, as will future believers. Our prayers—and the prayers of our students—reside in these bowls of heaven. They're making history as they hasten the coming of the kingdom and the King.

When I wrote *Youth Ministry on Your Knees* almost two decades ago, the two fresh prayer ministries, the International House of Prayer Kansas City and 24-7 Prayer, were just getting started. Both targeted youth. And both have grown into two of the largest prayer movements in the world. They are doing some serious bowl filling. As is The Cause and Contend, both offshoots of The Call, a little get-together of hundreds of thousands of young people on the Mall in Washington, D.C. which spread to stadium-filling events around the country the world.

Recently, revival broke out once again on the campus of Asbury University, quickly spreading across the street to Asbury Theological Seminary and across the country to scores of campuses. (By the time you read this, who knows what God could be doing in our midst?) One of the many amazing aspects of the Asbury revival was that over a year before it broke out, the annual Collegiate Day of Prayer was scheduled to be broadcast from Asbury University. Now that is heavenly timing! I watched the two-hour online broadcast, and wept throughout it. This is why:

A Faceless Generation

A couple decades ago, I was thumbing through a denominational magazine and stumbled across an article that grabbed my attention. The article included the manuscript of a commencement address given in 2000 to the graduating class of Simpson College by Lillian Poon, a Christian and Missionary Alliance pastor from the Bay Area. (Unfortunately, I cannot find this online; maybe you'll have better luck using AI!) A copy of the address has spent the past few decades hopping from year to year in my journal, where it serves as a powerful prophetic reminder and prayer guide. "A Faceless Generation" starts with this:

> Today God is raising up a faceless generation, a generation of believers who will seek only His glory, not their own. They are similar to the 144,000 that John described in Revelation: "They followed the Lamb wherever He goes" (Rev. 14:4). They are wired to sense Jesus only, hear His voice only and obey His commands only. They are single-minded in their following. They do not look to their left nor to their right. They follow Him so closely, you can only see the face of Jesus on them. Their names fade into the background. Their color and cultural distinctions are not recognizable.

After many years pondering and praying, I say with confidence, that generation is here. The faceless ones are among us—in our youth groups, on our volunteer teams, in our churches and ministries, and on the mission fields. They were at Asbury and the Collegiate Day of Prayer broadcast. Those entrusted with stewarding the Asbury revival took great pains to ensure Jesus was the only "celebrity" involved; the same was true for the Day of Prayer. In fact, the well-known names scheduled to speak at the Day of Prayer were conspicuously and gloriously absent at the broadcast.

For the past few years, about a dozen veteran youth workers have participated in Upper Zoom prayer calls on the first and third Thursdays of the month. The early morning call gathers Christians from across the country and across the pond. Most of us came to faith in Christ during the Jesus Revolution of the late 60s and early 70s. But our prayers are full of youthful passion and zeal. We often pray that we would have the privilege of witnessing another Jesus Revolution—whatever that might look like—in our lifetimes.

Perhaps between the time I'm writing this and when the completed book hits the market, a spiritual awakening or revival or whatever you want to call it will have begun. Our prayers, together with those of countless others, will have filled one of the heavenly bowls, and answers will come pouring down from heaven. Regardless, I'm convinced leaders of the next great move of God in youth ministry are among us. Their presence gives me great joy and hope.

A Call to Pray and Obey

Years ago I heard a sermon (on audio cassette!) by pastor Larry Lea from the National Symposium on the Post-Denominational Church. His message was titled, "Releasing the Prayer Anointing." In it, he described a meeting with the late Paul Yonggi Cho, who once pastored a little cell-based congregation of around 800,000 in South Korea. Larry met Pastor Cho, and was told in advance he would have a grand total of 20 seconds to ask him any question. When the time finally arrived, Larry blurted out something profound like, "What did you do to build such a large church?" To which Pastor Cho replied, "Pray, and obey. Ha Ha Ha Ha Ha!" Then Cho walked away. Absolutely epic. After feeling rather slighted, Lea realized the simple yet profound nature of Cho's comment. As I listened to the tape, I realized it as well.

Pastoring youth, serving with a youth organization, volunteering at a local church, or working at any job, it all boils down to praying and obeying, doesn't it? I know the multi-faceted Christian experience can't be reduced to just that. Bible study, corporate worship, discipleship, fasting, fellowship, memorization and meditation, sharing one's faith, and more, are integral and essential components. But doesn't living the Christian life depend to a large extent on hearing from God and living in obedience to what we hear?

Life can get out of control for most of us. Our current ministry is essentially a husband-and-wife operation. Keeping up with everything is quite a challenge, at times nearly more than I can manage. My to-be-filed drawer in my desk overflowed, so I bought a wire basket, overflowed that, overflowed a second one, and proceeded to a third basket. Phone calls and emails don't get returned as quickly as I would like; important notes get lost in the piles that have taken over my work space. My to-do list switches back and forth between an app on my smartphone and pages in my paper and pen planner, growing longer with each switch. I've got places to go, people to meet, ministry to do! In the midst of all this, I have come to the realization that my own gifting—I like to do multiple tasks and keep juggling a lot of balls—is not always an asset. One can only juggle so many balls before a few hit the ground.

Your life agenda is likely fleshed out differently than mine. But I sense we all, at times, share in this frustration. So, what's a person to do? Buy yet another wire basket? I don't think so. I know the answer is more complex than what I'm going to write next, but . . . pray and obey. We get marching orders, moment-by-moment, from the Father, and obey them. What Mary told the servants at the Cana wedding after the wine had run out, "Do whatever He tells you" (Jn. 2:5), is good advice for us all.

I want to be about the Father's business. I don't want to be about Mike's business. Sometimes the two match; sometimes not. But at this point in my life, and at this point in my efforts to reach a generation increasingly "harassed and helpless, like sheep without a shepherd" (Matt. 9:36), I don't have the luxury of hoping for a match. None of us do. As someone once said, "There is always enough time to do God's will." And so, increasingly, I pray and obey.

"Pray and obey" also applies in significant ways to what I do on assignment, be it speaking to students, facilitating a prayer summit, mentoring youth leaders, or even leading a house of prayer. I want to help youth workers and young people become men and women who know their Bibles, teach and practice biblical truth, share their faith, and live as light and salt in a dark, tasteless world. But if there is one persistent passion in what I do—if there is one persistent passion in what any of us who work with youth do—it should be to pray and obey. And to welcome the faceless ones populating our youth groups right now.

One more thing: "Ha Ha Ha Ha Ha!" A few laughs are good therapy.

Conclusion

A Final View from My Upper Room

At the beginning of this book, I mention numerous people who have had a significant influence on my pilgrimage as a follower of Jesus and man of prayer. They are not the only ones who have marked my life. In doing the final editing of this manuscript, I received word of another prominent Christian leader who is being investigated for possible moral failure. While all the high-profile leaders who have fallen grieve me deeply, this one cuts deeper than most. I am hoping it is fake news.

Beyond those who have made public headlines for the wrong reasons, the list of senior pastors, youth ministry mentors, and others I have personally looked up to and sought to emulate, but are no longer in ministry due to moral and/or ethical failures, is far, far too long. Of course, there shouldn't be a list at all! Yes, I understand that the biblical record is replete with men and women used by God mightily, yet with severe failings—Noah, Abraham, Jacob, Moses, Samson, David and Solomon, to mention just a few. I understand that our western church tendency to put leaders up on precarious pedestals is not healthy. And I very much understand the common proverb, "there, but for the grace of God, go I." As Paul wrote to the Corinthians, "So if you think you are standing firm, be careful that you don't fall" (1 Cor. 10:12).

Cumulatively, all this puts the fear of God in me. And that's a good thing! I'm in the fourth quarter of my earthly journey, and I want to finish well. But beyond that, I want my tribe of youth workers, old and young, to not just finish well, but to live each and every day in a manner that pleases God, attracts His blessing, and accelerates the advancing of the Kingdom and coming of the King.

The writer of Hebrews exhorts us, "Remember your leaders, who spoke the word of God to you. Consider the outcome of their way of life and imitate their faith" (Heb. 13:7). May all of us who belong this ragamuffin tribe of youth workers cultivate prayer prerequisites, give great attention to the development of our own prayer lives and those of the students we love, and encourage movements of corporate prayer for, and among, young people. And may the humility, holiness, and honesty of our lives be the apologetic that, along with bowls full of prayers and cutting-edge youth ministry praxis, ushers in a transformational move of God among young people! Maranatha!

One last word: Francis Frangipane is a pastor and prolific author who has greatly influenced me through his writings. In his book *The Shelter of the Most High*, he writes prophetically about the last days and the "simplicity and purity of devotion to Christ" that will be exhibited by believers. My prayer is that his description fits our tribe of youth workers, both now and in the future:

> "The earth's last great move of God shell be distinguished by an outpouring from Christ of irresistible desire for His people. To those who truly yearn for His appearing, there shall come, in ever-increasing waves, seasons of renewal from the presence of the Lord (see acts 3:19-21). Intimacy with Christ shall be restored to its highest level since the first century.
>
> Many on the outside of this move of God as well as those touched and healed by it will look and marvel, "How

did these common people obtains such power?" They will see miracles similar to when Jesus Christ walked the earth. Multitudes will be drawn into the valley of decision. For them, the kingdom of God will truly be at hand.

But for those whom the Lord has drawn to Himself, there will be no mystery as to how He empowered them. Having returned to the simplicity and purity of devotion to Christ, they will have received the baptism of love." (*The Shelter Of The Most High,* Charisma House, 2008. pg. 89)

Appendix

Books on Prayer

BECAUSE I'M A prayer guy, I used to have over 100 books on prayer in my library. I've since reduced my prayer library by 40 percent, and am continuing to streamline and simplify. One does not need so many books on prayer! Like I wrote earlier, the best way to grow in prayer is by doing it. That being said, I have learned a lot from those who have gone before me and written about it. So, as you build your own modest prayer library, here are some books I have found especially helpful.

Alves, Elizabeth. *Becoming A Prayer Warrior*. Renew, 1998.

Bounds, E. M. *Prayer and Revival*. Baker, 1993.

Brother Lawrence. *The Practice of the Presence of God*. Whitaker House, 1982.

Dawson, Joy. *Intercession, Thrilling and Fulfilling*. YWAM Publishing, 1997.

Duewel, Wesley. *Mighty Prevailing Prayer*. Zondervan, 1990.

Eastman, Dick. *The Hour That Changes the World*. Baker, 1978.

Foster, Richard. *Prayer: Finding The Heart's True Home*. Harper Collins, 1992.

Fuller, Cheri and Luce, Ron. *When Teens Pray*. Multnomah, 2002.

Greig, Pete. *God On Mute*. Regal Books, 2007.

Greig, Pete. *How To Hear God: A Simple Guide for Normal People*. NavPress, 2019.

Greig, Pete. *How to Pray: A Simple Guide for Normal People.* Zondervan, 2022.

Hawthorne, Steve and Kendrick, Graham. *Prayerwalking.* Creation House, 1993.

Madison, Carol. *Prayer That's Caught and Taught.* PrayerShop Publishing 2020.

Murray, Andrew. *Andrew Murray on Prayer.* Whitaker House, 1998.

Sacks, Cheryl. *Reclaim A Generation: 21 Days of Prayer for Schools.* PrayerShop Publishing, 2022.

Sheets, Dutch. *Intercessory Prayer.* Regal, 1996.

Staton, Tyler. *Praying Like Monks, Living Like Fools.* Zondervan, 2022.

About the Author

MIKE HIGGS has counted youth workers as his "tribe" for more than 45 years, and has served for 30+ years as "an advocate for prayer in the youth ministry movement, and an advocate for youth ministry in the prayer movement." He has worked for most of the major youth ministry organizations as a strategic prayer mobilizer and on-site prayer leader for big events and initiatives, facilitated dozens of youth worker prayer summits and retreats, taught and written widely on the topics of character and prayer, and continues to mentor the emerging generation of youth ministry leaders. He is the author of *Youth Ministry from the Inside Out* and *Youth Ministry on Your Knees,* as well as numerous monographs, booklets and published articles on prayer.

Mike is currently involved with the North American Prayer Summit, International Renewal Ministries, and International Prayer Connect. He is a founding member of the National Network of Youth Ministries. Along with his wife, Terri, Mike has served on America's National Prayer Committee for more than a quarter-century. They launched the Hailey House of Prayer in 2023, which is affiliated with the 24-7 Prayer movement. They also have deep relational roots in the IHOP-KC prayer movement.

Believing that prevailing prayer combined with civic service can lead to community transformation, Mike is actively engaged locally in civic affairs. He is the founder and president of the Carey-Picabo Chamber of Commerce, functions as a chaplain for many agencies in his county, and serves on the Boards of the Sun Valley Institute for Resiliency and Sun Valley Economic Development.

Mike and Terri are founding partners of sondance, an Idaho-based nonprofit that helps others to "dance with the Son." Their adult children Lilly and Levi live in Michigan and Idaho, respectively, with their spouses.